A DELICATE BALANCE

A DELICATE BALANCE

What Philosophy Can Tell Us
About Terrorism

TRUDY GOVIER

A Member of the Perseus Books Group

Copyright © 2002 by Westview Press, A Member of the Perseus Books Group

Westview Press books are available at special discounts for bulk purchases in the United States by corporations, institutions, and other organizations. For more information, please contact the Special Markets Department at the Perseus Books Group, 11 Cambridge Center, Cambridge MA 02142, or call (617) 252-5298.

Hardcover edition first published in 2002 in the United States of America by Westview Press, 5500 Central Avenue, Boulder, Colorado 80301-2877, and in the United Kingdom by Westview Press, 12 Hid's Copse Road, Cumnor Hill, Oxford OX2 9JJ

Paperback edition first published in 2004 by Westview Press.

Find us on the World Wide Web at www.westviewpress.com

The Library of Congress has catalogued the hardcover edition as follows:

Govier, Trudy.
  A delicate balance : what philosophy can tell us about terrorism /
Trudy Govier.
      p. cm.
Includes bibliographical references and index.
  ISBN 0-8133-6585-6 (hc)
  1. Terrorism—Moral and ethical aspects.   2. Violence—Moral and
ethical aspects.   3. September 11 Terrorist Attacks, 2001.   I. Title.
  BJ1459.5 .G68 2002
  172'.4—dc21

                                                            2002004932

ISBN 0-8133-4271-6 (pbk)

The paper used in this publication meets the requirements of the American National Standard for Permanence of Paper for Printed Library Materials Z39.48–1984.

10   9   8   7   6   5   4   3   2   1

CONTENTS

PREFACE

In this volume, I offer ethical reflections on the events of September 11, 2001, and their aftermath. As I write, works of political analysis proliferate, and the stories of the "war against terrorism" are surely not over. But reflecting on these themes remains important, and relatively few commentators have made values and philosophy central in their work.

As we struggle to come to terms with vulnerability and fear, we are exposed to a moral rhetoric of evil and justice and encouraged to cultivate a sense that we are engaged in a battle of good and evil. Some such appeals are manipulative and superficial, but others are heartfelt. All pose ethical and logical questions, pointing to a need for the moral reflection and logical evaluation that tend to be rare in times of crisis. I offer this volume as my own humble effort to address that need. The essays here express my conviction that sustainable security must be grounded in an appreciation of sound values and pursued by strategies that conform to those values. I have tried to write in an informal manner and avoid needless technicalities so that these essays will be accessible to readers from a wide variety of backgrounds.

I find the rhetoric of "evil" alarming, not because I don't believe that evil exists but rather because of its tendency to polarize and oversimplify. The notion that those who attack us are purely and simply evil discourages questioning and thought and suggests that we can save ourselves only by destroying evil others. I believe that is a dangerous illusion. I'm generally skeptical about military solutions to deep political conflicts. I believe that nonviolent solutions are always, in principle, preferable to violent ones and that if we constructed our institutions on that assumption, our capacity to resolve problems nonviolently would be far greater than it is today.

In the short term, a military approach to terrorism may protect us, but in the long term, we need to find solutions by pursuing education, development, dialogue, negotiation, and law. In such contexts, we can only be assisted by an appreciation of values and value differences, and the limitations of violence as a means of conflict resolution.

When we deal with issues of life and death, with responses to severe wrongdoing, with the justice of punishment and the credibility of international law, issues of values and ethics are far from irrelevant to the conduct of politics. On these matters, politics and ethics are inextricably connected; we are committed to a response that can be appraised in moral terms—whether we know it or not. Indeed, values are the core of the matter. Unreflective acceptance of orthodoxy does not remove us from the moral domain; it only means that we have supported other people's values by default. To think through our own principles and commitments requires questioning meanings, imagining alternatives, and understanding arguments. I've tried to portray those aspects of thinking in my reflections here, and I hope that readers will enjoy following my thinking even where they may dispute my conclusions.

I should like to acknowledge the warm support of Sarah Warner, Philosophy Editor at Westview Press; and the thoughtful energy of Sarah Goard-Baker, who assisted me with editing and research. For their comments and conversations about themes in this volume, I thank Anton Colijn, Caroline Colijn, Bev Delong, Doris Govier,

Peter and Marlene Fitzgerald-Moore, George Melnyk, Janet Sisson, and Wilhelm Verwoerd. For their frequent e-mail messages on topics pertinent to this book, I thank Barry Gan, Greg Moses, Bev Delong, and Richard Collins. It goes without saying that I am responsible for any errors of thought or presentation that remain.

The paperback version of this book went to press in the summer of 2004, providing an opportunity to update some of the material here. These observations are found in the notes at the end of each essay.

The invasion of Iraq in March 2003, the aftermath of that war, and the many debates before and after it have drawn public attention away from the situation in Afghanistan and even from the need to disempower al Qaeda and Osama bin Laden. Nevertheless, the 'war against terror' continues apace. The many dilemmas of security and human rights persist. Some six hundred men remain in U.S. custody at Guantanamo Bay where they have been held for two years with no charges laid against them. My sense is that all the topics explored here retain their relevance in the altered situation. Subsequent events have served only to strengthen my conviction that reconstruction is more demanding than military conquest, and for it, integrity and legitimacy are crucial.

TRUDY GOVIER
Calgary, Alberta, Canada

1

VULNERABILITY

Terrorist acts bring violence to ordinary people not normally central to a political conflict. And this, indeed, is usually their point: to intimidate by spreading shock, alarm, and fear. Before September 11, 2001, terrorism by foreign operatives was barely known on the North American continent. That its victims were people who had long assumed themselves safe made the impact all the greater because such death and destruction were not supposed to happen here. Commenting on the shock felt by North Americans, Archbishop Desmond Tutu alluded to a sense of bewilderment. North Americans were used to the idea that battles were waged thousands of miles away; so-called smart bombs were the weapons of choice, and other people's countries were the recipients. If "you've always been the top dog," you suddenly discover your vulnerability and profound shock will be the result, Tutu said. It's as though you're thinking, "'Hey, I'm just like any other human being. We are like any other human society. We're vulnerable. Vulnerable.'"

So far as mundane safety goes, North Americans have been a privileged group. Terrible events such as political bombings, amputations, and disappearances happened in countries far away. Even the nuclear threat felt remote and unreal to most people most of the time. These things weren't supposed to happen, not at all, and they certainly weren't supposed to happen here.

The actions of September 11 inspire a special kind of fear because the victims were proceeding with their everyday work lives. We have a sense of acute vulnerability: It could happen to anyone. Even you. Even me. The perpetrators of this terror are fearful men who will go to their own deaths to attack Western culture. If you set off on a journey to attend a wedding or market a product, you could board a vehicle that somebody turns into a weapon of mass destruction. What was supposed to be a pleasant little trip could make you part of somebody else's suicidal attack. If you work in a tall building, retrieving a document from your office or preparing your hair salon for the next shampoo could be your last action before you leap from a window to escape raging fires, only to plunge a hundred stories to your death.

In the aftermath of the September 11 attacks, travel is no longer fun to contemplate. It's a stressful prospect. We no longer just hear planes; the noise of a plane recalls images of fire and terror. High buildings look vulnerable and remind us of calamity. Box cutters are frightful objects. The needles of a diabetic, even paper clips or eyebrow tweezers, could become tools that help turn an airplane into a weapon of mass destruction. Artificial sweetener and baby powder might contain anthrax spores. Previously an object of interest, hand-addressed mail has become a potential hazard to be approached with care. For some, every Arabic name, even every brown face, poses a threat. Our position in the world is upset because what was mundane is no longer so. And airplanes flying into buildings is not the only form terrorism could take. You could breathe in toxic fumes, consume poisoned food or medications, or drink water that has been deliberately contaminated by your enemies. These aren't pleasant thoughts.

Security can be stepped up by hiring more people and staging even more thorough inspections in a host of contexts, but it's an illusion to think that every hole can be blocked. Developing the theme, analyst David Carr commented that the United States offers especially tempting prospects for terrorists. Fifty of the world's one hundred tallest buildings; the Mall of America in Minneapolis (the world's largest shopping mall); and the Indianapolis Motor Speedway, which can seat more than 250,000 people, are just some of the targets Carr cites.

Terrorism threatens us deeply because it puts into question our ordinary lives and the trust we need to conduct them. Our vulnerability stems from our interdependence; we are linked together profoundly in our need for the basic items of life. Nearly all the trivial objects of our lives have come in contact with thousands of other people. If someone wanted to alter a vehicle, poison the water, amend a pharmaceutical formula, spray crops with toxins, destroy a bridge, or put explosives inside his shoes—well, how could we stop him from doing so? Especially if he were willing to lose his own life in the process? For many North Americans, the fundamental factor in changes after September 11 is the spread of fear. What was mundane can no longer be so; what we took for granted for so many years, we can presume no longer.

The interdependence of human beings in complex modern societies is nothing new: there was plenty of interdependence before September 11, 2001. Human beings have long depended on each other for food, shelter, and clothing. For love and intimacy, friendship, collegiality, and neighborly assistance. For communications, information, expertise, and advice. At deeper levels, we depend on each other for our understanding of the world, for basic knowledge, and ultimately for language and reasoning itself. In leading our own lives, we need other people, and we depend on them. In our daily lives, we implicitly trust other people, far more people than we realize, most of them strangers. We have unconscious but deep expectations that mundane objects are reliable; we don't, for instance, expect people to poison the mail, set fire to their shoes, contaminate the water, or turn themselves into flying and walking bombs. Our social trust works for us because most people act reasonably well most of the time. They do their jobs with a fair degree of conscientiousness and competence, in moderate pursuit of their own interests while giving due consideration to others. And we don't notice our vulnerability when things go on as expected. The reliable and good—the ordinary day at the office, the flight that arrives on time, the grilled cheese sandwich that tastes pretty good, the mail that is opened without effect—are normal and unremarked. It's the surprising and damaging events that make the news.

The range of social trust extends far beyond the obvious because so many of the mundane *things* that we take for granted are artifacts produced by human beings. Fundamentally, it is people who are the objects of our trust; when we rely on things in the normal way, we are implicitly trusting the other people who provided them. This means trusting other people for their competence; we presume these people know what they are doing and how to do it. It also means trusting them for their motivation; we presume they are not trying to maim or kill us—and that's the presumption that terrorists make us question. Social trust is fundamental in life and it's the upheaval of social trust that makes terrorist attacks so profoundly disturbing. They provide such appallingly clear evidence that things are not all right with our world. Sociologists sometimes say that trust is the glue that holds society together. An almost invisible web of confident reliance underlies mundane life that, in normal times, tends to go unnoticed. We become aware of that reliance and our casual confidence only when things begin to go wrong. You could say that terrorism poisons the social glue, inspiring fear that it just won't stick any longer. When you stop to think about it, terrorists could operate nearly anywhere. A taxi? Didn't one of those hijackers work for a while as a taxi driver? Your cup of tea? Who had access to the water used to make it? That polite young man at the Xerox machine? He might be making false documents to support somebody who wants to launch another attack.

We have always been vulnerable. The difference terrorism makes is that we have become aware of our vulnerability. People who seek to destroy us could do so in thousands of ways; and many thousands of people hate us and want to destroy what they hate. Our old presumptions of confidence and security are gone, which is why the world seems so different now.

Political leaders tell us to be vigilant and urge us to report "anything suspicious" to authorities. The problem is that just about anything could be suspicious, given the right context and assumptions. Vigilance; we should be vigilant, authorities tell us. But against whom and why? These same authorities are advising that people should not be prejudiced against Arabs or Muslims. But then, who should we watch? Middle-aged matrons? Frail elderly gentlemen? Blond teenagers? Could such people be bribed or coerced into collaborating with terrorists? Could they be the dupes of terrorists? The idea that a white American-looking person might be a terrorist sympathizer is not only imaginable, it's a reality: John Walker Lindh, a middle-class youth from California, fought with the Taliban in Afghanistan and had trained in al-Qaeda terrorist camps to improve his skills. There's also April Ray, an American brought up as a Muslim in Tucson, Arizona, and described in a recent news article as "a suburban Dallas housewife." Ray is married to Wadih al-Hage, who was for several years a secretary to Osama bin Laden and is now serving a life sentence for conspiracy to commit terrorism in the August 1998 bombings of two U.S. embassies in East Africa. Ray tells of picnicking on the banks of the Blue Nile with the families of other radical Islamists. She was under the impression that bin Laden was a kind person and a good employer.

The advice to be vigilant seems confusingly vague; it conveys the general idea that we are supposed to be vigilant but does not tell us what we should attend to. Completely generalized vigilance would be paranoia, if it were possible at all; and surely life cannot go on this way. The same leaders who warn us to be vigilant also tell us to go on with our ordinary lives. We must not be intimidated even though we're shocked and frightened. A delicate balance of fear and confidence seems to be required. We have to watch out, but we also have to go on with our lives.

Human beings have an extraordinary drive and capacity to continue with ordinary life. During the long and vicious civil war in Lebanon in the 1980s, television news broadcasts showed scenes of ordinary Lebanese people carrying on with their lives—somehow. I was always moved by the scenes of laundry hanging out to dry because they provided such a homely background to the smoke and gunfire. Bombs, killings, terror, mayhem, and madness; and yet someone had done the family laundry. People lived in Beirut. They cooked supper and washed the dishes, and no doubt many went to their jobs as usual, to support themselves and their families, during the bitter civil war. Life goes on. In Sarajevo in the mid-1990s, snipers on the hillsides made every excursion risky. Still, the beleaguered people of Sarajevo conducted their lives in the middle of all this. They shopped for bread, met in cafes, read stories to their children, went shopping, kept diaries, and made love.

But it's a sure thing that North Americans are no less resilient and determined than other people. Like others around the world, we crave, and we have a tremendous ability to go on with life while somehow accepting our vulnerability, reconciling confidence and vigilance, and constructing a new sense of the normal.

As I thought about people who cope in turbulent times, my mind turned to the later Stoics, who lived under the depraved and mad emperor Nero in the first century C.E. Nero should probably get some credit for later Stoicism: The terrifying nature of his rule must have added considerably to the appeal of the doctrine. Stoic philosophy can be interpreted as proposing a solution to the problems of vulnerability and fear. You could think of Stoic works almost as "how to" books surviving from the dangerous Roman world. Under the tyranny of corrupt and erratic emperors, people could be subjected to chains, torture, exile, and sudden execution. Epictetus the Stoic was a slave who somehow received an education and won his personal freedom. After philosophers were expelled from Rome in 89 C.E., he began teaching at Nicopolis.

The central idea of the Stoics was to distinguish firmly between what is in our power and what is not. In our power, they said, are opinions, beliefs, attitudes, desires, aversions, and our own acts. Not in our power are the body, parts of the body, parents, brothers, sisters, children, property, status, reputation, and the acts of other people—especially the rulers of society. The secret of human happiness is to care only about those things that are within our power. "Who then is invincible? It is he whom none of the things disturbs which are independent of the will," Epictetus said. We cannot control our perceptions and impressions, or our original impulsive emotions. But we can control our responses to them. The Stoics saw human beings as creatures of will, and they counseled the need for a strong, steady purpose. We have a freedom of choice about how we reflect and act, and we can discipline ourselves to limit our vulnerability. The Stoics counseled that we could achieve tranquillity by using our reason and defining the good in terms of things that depend on the will. Desires should be carefully reined in. If you've got an expensive new car, replace it with a slightly battered old one; then you'll be less vulnerable to car theft. Your car won't tempt many thieves, but if anyone were to steal it, your loss would be modest and you'd be less affected by it. Epictetus said, "I must die. Must I then die lamenting? I must be put in chains. Must I then also lament?" Death and misfortune are inevitable, but lamenting is not—that was his point. There is no country in which he could live, Epictetus said, where death would not someday befall him. But he could control his feelings and attitudes about his death, and that's something worth doing. We can learn to discipline our desire and exercise our will, Epictetus advised. And Philosophy will be our teacher.

Difficulties arise when we consider the fundamental Stoic distinction between what is within our power and what is not; for the Stoics it was all a question of control. It's a tempting model, especially when we're feeling vulnerable, because control would indeed be a wonderful thing to have. But thinking about control or non-control is an oversimplification. There is also such a thing as influence. For all that we cannot control our children, we do, surely, influence them in many ways. In Western societies, people have some chance, at least, of influencing political leaders and officials. The belief that either things are subject to our control or they are not ignores certain realities; in the end, it's a discouraging dichotomy because it omits the idea that we might exert influence in contexts where we don't have full control.

The Stoics believed that Nature would provide the ultimate ethical guide for men and women. Nature is reasonable; we can study it and come to grasp its laws, and when we do, we will learn the ethical principles we need to guide us. The Nature that grounded late Stoicism was fatalistic. What was going to be was going to be; it was terrible; people had to adjust to it and cope. They could determine their attitudes and emotions because those, and those alone, were within the power of will and reason. As for anything else, the idea was to train yourself not to care. You couldn't do anything about your physical vulnerability, but you could make yourself emotionally invulnerable. The Stoics coped with their fearful world by trying to organize their emotions so that they cared only about the few things that were within their control. Western readers, few of whom adopt a fatalistic stance on the world, are likely to find problems in such conceptions. Faced with vulnerability, we would prefer to limit it rather than accept it as an inevitable fact about modern life.

If Epictetus and his colleagues had written a "how to" book for the aftermath of September 11, they would have advised us to organize our lives so that we understand what fate holds for us; we would then be able to correct our emotions according to our beliefs and cope calmly with the inevitable. Such a book would have been a hard sell. *Que Sera Sera* was a popular song in the 1950s, but few Westerners would accept the refrain that "whatever will be will be" in a serious context. Fatalism is profoundly unmodern—and modernism profoundly unfatalistic.

Modern Judaeo-Christian frameworks incorporate some version of free will that theologians seek to reconcile with the Creation and the power of God. Scientifically, the understanding represented in physical theory shows gaps in explanation and arguably in causation itself. Political and social reality seem less predictable than physical reality, and physical reality itself has unpredictable dimensions. Surprises can happen, and some surprises are catastrophes. But others offer unexpected opportunities and provide a basis for hope.

I found Stoic writings a delightful distraction in the weeks after the attacks of September 11. But if we're looking for a complete philosophical answer to our questions about fear and vulnerability, the Stoics can't provide it because their thinking is too fatalistic to fit our own. Even so, I think that Epictetus stated some simple but useful truths. Our attitudes are our own, and so are our feelings. We can amend these feelings according to reason and we can improve our reason by paying close attention to what's happening—even when the information is unpleasant. Our feelings and values can be altered on reflection. Not everything is worth caring about. Many luxuries are dispensable.

Most significantly, the story of Epictetus is just one among thousands that show people in other times and places coping with chaos and vulnerability; while conducting meaningful lives in their worlds of terrifying confusion.

Notes

Desmond Tutu's remarks were in Washington, D.C., on November 4, 2001, in an interview by Akwe Amosu of allafrica.com. I traced them at http://www. africapolicy.org/doct()1/tutu/()111.htm. The discussion of trust and vulnerability is based on my own earlier work in *Social Trust and Human Communities*

(Montreal and Kingston: McGill-Queen's University Press, 1997). Details from David Carr are taken from his essay, "The Futility of 'Homeland Defense,'" which appeared in *Atlantic Monthly* in January 2002. April Ray's story is told by Kevin Peraino and Evan Thomas in "Odyssey Into Jihad," *Newsweek,* January 14, 2002. Quotations from Epictetus are from *The Discourses of Epictetus, with the Encheiridion and Fragments,* ed. and trans. George Long (A. L. Burt Company) (no city or date of publication available). Background information on the Stoics is taken from William L. Davidson, *The Stoic Creed* (New York: Arno Press, 1979).

2

VICTIMS

In recent years, moralists and commentators have paid considerable attention to victims and the impact of serious wrongs. Discussions of posttraumatic stress, counseling, public apologies, civil suits, redress, memorials, truth commissions, and war crimes trials have been common themes of late. Some commentators have offered the cynical observation that during the 1990s, the prospect of a new millennium was motivating people to shed the sins of the past. Others bemoaned trendy repentance, speaking sarcastically of an "Age of Apology," and implying that victims were exploiting their victimhood. In most contexts, I didn't feel that way. I believe that the needs and situations of victims should be taken seriously, that sympathy for them is commendable, and that apologies, reparations, and memorials make a lot of sense. Nevertheless, it's possible to go too far and create a kind of Myth of Victimhood that portrays victims as pure beings who possess a special moral authority as a result of their injuries. The Myth of Victimhood is especially hazardous when the world's most conspicuous victim is the world's one remaining superpower.

What is a victim? We speak loosely about the victims of tidal waves, or earthquakes, or disease. But in the context of terrorism and violence, being a victim is more specific. A victim is one who is injured, killed, or harmed by acts of violence committed by perpetrators in pursuit of their political goals. Victims are the wronged parties who were innocuously and innocently going about their business when dreadful harm was brought upon them. Perpetrators are the agents of that harm.

An estimated 3,100 people died as a result of the September 11 attacks on the World Trade Center and the Pentagon. But that's only the first level of victimhood. There are also secondary victims—the families and close friends of those who were killed or injured. People posting signs in New York, hoping against hope that their loved ones had survived; people weeping, mourning, grieving, struggling with children, trying somehow to go on. And clearly, it doesn't stop there. A whole community was affected. New Yorkers who didn't lose a family member or close friend were also victims of these attacks. Dust, fire, smoke, chemicals, confusion, fear, anxiety—these affected just about everyone in the New York community. Community members harmed by the effects of the attacks constitute a third level of victims.

The effects went further still. The United States as a whole was affected by fear, anxiety, economic loss, sorrow, and a sense of vulnerability and dislocation. We can define a fourth level of victims following the individual, the family, and the community: that of the nation. It's estimated that some 100,000 jobs were lost as a result of the September 11 attacks. And even that is not the end because there were many adverse effects outside the United States. People and governments in allied nations were shocked and sympathetic. First, they shared horror and pain; later, a sense of their own sense of vulnerability and insecurity. Then came the broader impact: their military and intelligence obligations, their economies and economic interdependence, their immigration and civil rights policies—it goes on.

Five levels if you keep counting; but the point is not so much to count levels as it is to appreciate how the effects spiral out from the initial events clustered in their center of pain and damage. The spreading happens in time as well as space: We can be sure that such effects will long outlast the original deed. More than fifty years after the Second World War, people in Europe, North America, the Middle East, and elsewhere are still living with effects on a spiral of victims.

On the scale of nonstate terrorist attacks, those of September 11 were the largest ever. By comparison, intermittent terrorism in Northern Ireland claimed the lives of some 3,000 persons over thirty years, and the three years of struggle between Israel and the Palestinians (1998–2001) claimed approximately 3,600. On the other hand, there are more deaths from causes less dramatic than terrorist acts. UNICEF calculates that some 36,000 children die every day from hunger and malnutrition-related diseases; and the UN estimates that 500,000 to 1 million people have died in Iraq from hunger and disease attributable to ten years of sanctions against the regime of Saddam Hussein.

From the moral point of view, all lives, and all deaths, are equal, because the significance of a death arises from the intrinsic dignity and value of human life itself. There is no distinguishing feature about a person—beauty, intelligence, knowledge, citizenship, or geography—that makes his or her death of greater or lesser moral significance than any other. But media attention appears to make some deaths count more than others, and that selectivity can distort our thinking. Many killed in the World Trade Center were well educated and economically powerful, agents at the center of the global economy, citizens of the world's one remaining superpower. They were inhabitants of the richest city in the world—and a center of Western media empires. In conjunction with the enormous and visible drama of the attacks, these facts ensured that the deaths received enormous attention. Because these people and this place were what they were, the effects of the devastation were unusually far-flung politically and economically. The events of September 11 were shocking and dramatic; the people were "our kind of people";

their vulnerability proved to be our vulnerability; and they were located at the center of a vast media empire. The coverage was intense. And the challenges, obviously, new. The victims deserve sympathy, but when we extend it to them, we may forget about victims elsewhere.

The bombing of Afghanistan by the United States and Britain initiated another spiral of victims: more violence, deaths, suffering relatives, communities torn apart, hungry refugees in the thousands. And all this among people who lived in desperate conditions before it all began. Terrorists in training at camps, Osama bin Laden and his associates, and members of the Taliban regime that sheltered them may be regarded as perpetrators. Afghan citizens who supported the Taliban regime might arguably be so regarded if they knew that the regime was harboring terrorists and accepting support from them. But most civilians in Afghanistan were surely innocent of any wrongdoing in the matter; these people were not perpetrators. The perpetrators of the September 11 violence were the nineteen hijackers themselves. But the matter does not stop there, because other people must have been behind these attacks, facilitating their planning and coordination, colluding with necessary deceptions, supplying resources, and supporting and perpetrating an ideology of hatred and martyrdom in the name of Islam. So it is for any instance of organized violence. Those who rationalize it, argue for it, incite it, plan it, and pay for it share responsibility with those who are its actual agents.

As is the case with other serious wrongs, victim and perpetrator spirals extend widely in space and endure long in time. Eventually, the distinction between victims and perpetrators may start to seem fuzzy. Do U.S. citizens and those of other Western countries share responsibility for sanctions on Iraq and for the deaths of Iraqi children? Can these deaths be regarded as killings? Are we, to some degree, perpetrators to the third or fourth degree in this and similar cases? Critics of U.S. policy would no doubt argue that there is a sense in which some victims in New York perpetrated wrongs against dissidents in Saudi Arabia—homeland of fifteen of the nineteen hijackers—and even in some sense against the hijackers themselves. In that country, for some fifty years, an oppressive regime has been supported by the U.S. government in exchange for guaranteed oil supplies. It's arguable that U.S. citizens who have failed to oppose this affiliation and supported their government's foreign policy in various ways share responsibility for the nature and actions of the Saudi regime.

Perhaps every person is in some ways a victim and in others a perpetrator. Would that mean that the distinction between victims and perpetrators loses its moral significance? Would it show that the appalling wrongs of history and policy cancel each other out in the long run? That we should forget about all those wrongs? That's what some critics of the Age of Apology had begun to think before September 11.

The truth is, though, you can be a faultless victim of one crime while bearing or sharing responsibility for others. Being in the right in one context doesn't cancel out being wrong in another; people can be perpetrators in one context and victims in another; and when they are victims, their having been perpetrators doesn't subtract from their victimhood. Fundamentally, at stake here is the assumption that victims must be morally pure. These are the grieving survivors, injured and shocked, struggling to continue their lives in the wake of a horribly unanticipated tragedy. To criticize these suffering people seems beyond all moral etiquette. They are the injured ones, the ones who need our help. And it is positively offensive to say anything against them or anyone else acting on their behalf. Critics of the bombing of Afghanistan by U.S. and U.K. forces were met with the comment, "Tell that to the people in Manhattan."

We are not victims or perpetrators in an absolute sense, but with reference to some particular act or event; this is just to say that whether we are victims or perpetrators depends on the context.

Those who died in the attacks of September 11 were genuinely victims; they did not plan or carry out the attacks, they were not perpetrators, and they were not morally responsible for the attacks on themselves. These people were innocent parties, individuals going about their daily business and involved by bad luck in a deep conflict between the West and elements of a radical and murderous version of fundamentalist Islam. But that is not to deny that some persons among the victims may have been perpetrators, in other contexts, of other wrongs. Some victims may have supported exploitative foreign policies. Some may have been bankers who colluded to impose harsh monetary policies having drastic implications for health and educational services. Some may have been racists. Or embezzlers. Or cheaters, sexual harassers, disloyal husbands or wives. It's a matter of context—and context removes the halo that has come to surround *victims* and *victimhood*.

According to the Myth of Victimhood, victims are uniquely special beings who are pure and innocent, have a unique moral authority, and are above criticism. Complications about context and shared responsibility throw doubt on the first element here— the assumption of *Innocence*. The idea is that Victims are wholly innocent, morally pure, and can do no wrong. The fallacy, obviously, lies in the transference from one context to others. To be innocent in the context of a crime committed against you doesn't guarantee your innocence in other contexts.

A second element in the Myth of Victimhood is the notion that victims enjoy a special Moral Authority. This is the principle that the victims of a wrong are the persons who best understand how to respond to its aftermath. The Myth of Moral Authority gets started because we confuse one sort of knowledge with another and come to suppose that suffering gives people expertise on other matters, such as foreign and defense policy. Victims best understand their own suffering and loss—and no observer or "expert" should pretend to tell them what their own experiences are. Their suffering does give them a special kind of understanding, the knowledge of what it is like to experience this particular pain and loss and to cope, day after day, in tragic circumstances. Louise Kurtz, for example, suffered burns to 70 percent of her body when she was a victim of the attack on the Pentagon. All her fingers had to be amputated. This woman must have experienced terrible pain, and her rehabilitation is likely to be enormously difficult. Her husband praised her as a "pillar of strength"—and that is what she will need to be, for the loss of those fingers means that she is going to be seriously handicapped for the rest of her life. We who are lucky enough to take our fingers for granted can only guess how difficult it would be to manage without them and how disturbing to face the prospect of adapting to such a loss. As a victim, Louise Kurtz certainly deserves our deepest sympathy. Her feelings should be honored and respected, as should those of any victim. But that doesn't make her an expert on other matters.

The Myth of Moral Authority presents problems when we confuse suffering with practical knowledge about policy issues. Issues arise about responding to wrongdoers: how, when, where, by what means, to what effect, and with what justice? Issues arise about victims themselves: Which forms are best for acknowledgment, compensation, and repair? And there are further issues about restoring a physical environment and establishing appropriate memorials. Victims are likely to gain a deep understanding from their suffering, and that understanding may provide them wisdom about their own pain and how to cope with their own lives. But such experience doesn't amount to practical knowledge about policy. A widow may know better than others what it is to lose her husband and provide for sad little children alone, but that doesn't mean she's equipped to advise on civil societies, military campaigns, or international legal institutions. Nor does widowhood make her an expert on the complexities of compensation: who should get what from whom, and why. Suffering is suffering and policy is policy; knowing what it is to suffer doesn't make a person an expert on policy.

In foreign and defense policy, for example, much is at stake. Because historical, political, tactical, and ethical understanding are all relevant to crucial decisions, many different voices and perspectives are needed to make good decisions. The sentiments of victims are relevant, but they are not the only factors; and respect for them can take us only so far.

The limitations of the Myth of Moral Authority are readily apparent when we recognize that there are many victims. Since these victims often disagree with each other, they can't all be right. After September 11, many victims supported harsh military reprisal, but others advocated nonviolent responses. Some people walked from New York to Washington, D.C., to protest the military campaign in Afghanistan; later, they formed a Peaceful Tomorrow group that drew its name from Martin Luther King's statement that "Wars are poor chisels for carving out peaceful tomorrows." Others traveled to Kabul to share their sorrow with injured and grieving Afghan civilians. Victims also disagreed among themselves about the administration of compensation packages and the appropriateness of various types of memorials at the World Trade Center site. Suffering and sorrow are profound bonds, but they don't end disputes or undermine the fundamental logical point that when people disagree they can't all be right.

A third element in the Myth of Victimhood is a corollary of the notion of Authority. This is the matter of *Deference*—the supposition that one should not criticize victims. Deference got some critics of U.S. foreign policy into big trouble in the aftermath of the September 11 attacks. Sunera Thobani is a professor who claimed in a speech she made in October 2001 that the United States has a foreign policy "soaked in blood" and has committed "horrific violence," so much so that it is "the largest and most dangerous global force in the world." Observers were shocked that anyone would criticize the United States in this way so soon after the attacks. After all, the country had become a victim of horrifying devastation, there was still anxiety about anthrax contaminating the mail, and people were feeling fearful and vulnerable. This was surely no context in which to criticize the United States! As a result of her speech, Thobani was labeled a foreign imposter and a hate monger; prodded by a caller, the police considered charging her with a hate crime. Thobani's problems stem from the notion of Deference, which stipulates that those who are not victims should not presume to criticize those who are. To do so is worse than tactless; it is offensive and morally wrong.

But Deference has to be resisted, I think. To be sure, we should respect victims and honor their suffering, but such respect should not give them the last word on policy issues. Those issues are highly complex and reasonable judgments are hard to come by. Informed debate requires many voices. We can ask that critics defer to victims by showing them respect and courtesy, but we cannot demand their silence.

In early November 2001 when the bombing of Afghanistan had gone on for about a month, some were beginning to question its effectiveness. The military effort was expensive; bombing was devastating an already poor country; innocent civilians were losing their homes and their lives. At that stage, it looked as if the Taliban were peculiarly immovable; in addition, the U.S. State Department had inadvertently contributed to a mood of disenchantment by confessing that, for all its rhetoric about bringing evildoers to justice, Osama bin Laden might just manage to elude capture indefinitely. Doubts were expressed in many quarters, including—notably—some European capitals. Was the bombing doing any good? Should it be continued?

Seeking to consolidate support, the British prime minister, Tony Blair, addressed the problem in a fervent speech. He said, in essence, "Remember the victims. Remember the attacks on September 11, how terrible they were, how many people suffered and how terribly, how we mourned and what we went through. Don't ever forget."

Blair was right and wrong about victims. He was right when he implied that the victims had been wronged in horrible crimes. He was right when he implied that they deserve our respect and sympathy. But he was wrong when he appealed to the victims' suffering as a way of justifying the bombing campaign. We should always respect victims and their suffering, but that respect won't tell us what to do next. In his rhetorical zeal, Blair lapsed into the Myth of Victimhood.

Notes

In the spring of 2002, hundreds more died in a cycle of suicide bomb attacks and Israeli army retaliations. Precise numbers of deaths were not known when this book went to press.

Sunera Thobani is a Women's Studies professor at the University of British Columbia. Her speech and the reaction to it were described in the *Globe and Mail* for October 24, 2001. Thobani explained her stance in an e-mail message circulated on November 14, 2001. The story of Louise Kurtz may be found in *U.S. News and World Report,* December 10, 2001. The American widows' visit to Kabul was covered on the British Broadcasting Corporation international news broadcast on January 15, 2002. The women were shown talking with Afghan civilians in a shattered house; presumably, a translator was present. The war took a very different turn shortly after this essay was written. But the Myths of Victimhood persist.

As of the winter of 2004, hundreds more had died, on both sides of the Israeli-Palestinian conflict, in a seemingly endless cycle of suicide bomb attacks and Israeli army retaliations.

Sunera Thobani is a Women's Studies professor at the University of British Columbia. Her speech and the reaction to it were described in the *Globe and Mail* for October 24, 2001. Thobani explained her stance in an e-mail message circulated on November 14, 2001. Between the fall of 2001 and the winter of 2004, many other critics of U.S. policy were deemed anti-American and insufficiently sympathetic to victims. Their number includes Noam Chomsky, Susan Sontag, Gore Vidal, Paul Krugman, and Arundhati Roy.

The story of Louise Kurtz appeared in *U.S. News and World Report,* December 10, 2001. The story of the American widows' visit to Kabul was covered on the British Broadcasting Corporation international news broadcast on January 15, 2002. The women were shown talking with Afghan civilians in a shattered house; presumably a translator was present. The war in Afghanistan took a different turn soon after this essay was written, and the Taliban regime was defeated. As of January 2004, there was considerable physical insecurity in that country outside Kabul. Warlords exerted power in some areas, and there was sporadic fighting between U.S. and allied forces and the Taliban and remnants of al Qaeda.

The Myths of Victimhood have not died—though, so far as September 11 victims are concerned, their force has been diminished somewhat by subsequent events including, especially, the invasion of Iraq and subsequent struggles there.

3

EVIL

On November 9, 2001, George W. Bush addressed the United Nations on the terrorist threat. During the question period following his address, someone asked him whether Osama bin Laden possessed nuclear weapons. Bush dodged the question, saying the only thing he knew about bin Laden was that he was an evil person.

According to the president, the hijackers were evildoers; those who sponsored them were also evil. And their deeds were the evil acts of evil men. Evil must be eradicated; hence the global war against this dastardly force that would destroy civilization. The use of "evil" in political discourse is by no means unique. President Ronald Reagan once referred to the Soviet Union as an "evil empire." During the height of the conflict between Iran and the United States, Iranians used to refer to the United States as "the great Satan"; they meant, presumably, that the United States was such a force of evil in the world that it was serving Satan himself. And not metaphorically.

There is a theological sound to such statements, and one might think that to understand evil we need recourse to theologians who will explain how and why God and the Devil contend on this earth for supremacy. In theological terms, evil men might be understood as acting on behalf of the supernatural forces of wickedness, personified, perhaps, in the Devil himself. Evil means that the acts of these people serve Satan and are contrary to the purposes of God and the forces of Good. Given the president's religious beliefs, it may be that he understands "evil" in this way; Osama bin Laden and his cohorts act with the Devil to oppose the forces of Good.

Evil. Wickedness. Sin. Concepts often used and appealed to, concepts that can have their uses even in the public discourse of secular societies. Yet they call for explanation. What is evil? What makes an act so bad that it can correctly be referred to as evil? What does it mean to be an evil person? An evil state? Are all evil people or states absolutely, permanently, irretrievably evil?

Public discourse is supposed to be, well, public, and modern liberal societies insist upon a separation of church and state. People adhere to different faiths and theologies, different interpretations of the relationship between religious faith and moral beliefs, different notions of how law and politics should mesh with religion and morality. Many hold no religious beliefs, being atheists or agnostics. Despite an influential Judaeo-Christian heritage, Western liberal societies are designed to allow for all these differences.

When religious differences underlie a political conflict, appealing to one's own particular theology is especially risky. It risks turning the conflict into some kind of holy war. President Bush didn't want to move in that direction. To build an international coalition that included Muslim countries, it was crucial for U.S. leaders to portray the struggle as one between terrorists (evil) and civilization (good), and not as a struggle between Islam (evil) and Christianity (good).

In any event, when it comes to evil, the enlightenment to be extracted from theology is less than one might think. For thousands of years, philosophers and theologians have struggled with the problem of evil in the context of God's power and creation. In these discussions, it was common to distinguish between natural evil and moral evil. Natural evils were serious misfortunes that befell people as a result of natural events such as earthquakes, tidal waves, and epidemics; whereas moral evil was a feature of human actions and agents. (Natural evil will seem evil only if we believe in a supernatural power that is responsible for these natural catastrophes.) The classic problem of evil is this: If God is all-good and all-powerful, that should mean He could prevent evil of both kinds. So why does He allow evil to exist? So many good people suffer from natural evils like cancer and tidal waves, yet so many bad people skip through life with impunity, accumulating fortune as they go. So many bad people commit cruel acts such as battery and sexual abuse and never suffer punishment; at the same time, so many good people suffer, so excruciatingly, the effects of the wrongful things these bad people do. If God exists and is all-powerful, why does He permit such things to go on? The knot is still discussed.

To take an especially extreme case, why did God allow the Holocaust to happen? It was clearly evil on a massive scale; yet if God exists, God must have permitted it to occur.

The eighteenth-century philosopher Gottfried Leibniz offered consolation to the afflicted in the form of a proof that evil does not exist, not when we fully understand how things that appear to be evil fit into the world. To get through the proof, you have to assume that God exists and God is a Being who acts on reasons. Only good reasons. According to Leibniz, that means God never does anything unless He has a Sufficient Reason for doing so. He created the world, which He could have done only if He had a Sufficient Reason for doing so. That means this world must be the best of all possible worlds; were it not so, God would not have had Sufficient Reason for creating it. He would have created another world instead. Given that this world of ours does exist, it must be the best of all possible worlds. Thus it contains no evil. What appears to be evil is needed for the whole, and is good, and could be understood to be so if we possessed complete knowledge.

Innocent children dying of abuse and neglect by their own parents; women burned to death for providing inadequate dowries;

hurricanes destroying the painfully tended crops of struggling farmers; idealistic activists struck down in the prime of life by disease; loving mothers and fathers killed by terrorists: if we understood such things fully, we would realize that they are not evil in the end. Or so proclaims Leibniz. These things happen in our world; they are needed elements in the unfolding of this world. Because they are needed they are not in the final sense evil but only seem to be so from our limited perspective. And because the world must (by philosophical proof) be the best of all possible worlds, what seems to be evil is not really so. In the end (somehow) all is for the best. Accusing God of permitting evil is an arrogant presumption that implies we understand God's purposes and the nature of the moral world He has created. According to Leibniz, evil is ultimately unreal.

Few who have felt the agony of human suffering or have the imagination to understand it will be convinced by such arguments. And if they are not, they are in good company. Moved by the deaths of some 50,000 people in the Lisbon earthquake of 1755, Voltaire wrote *Candide* to satirize Leibnizian optimism. In *Candide,* a favorite in its own time and later to become a 1950s Broadway musical, an innocent young hero and his woman friend are exposed to appalling cruelty. Robbery, abduction, running the gauntlet, rape, torture, inquisition. And, of course, war on many sides. Such horrors were not purely inventions of Voltaire's imagination; unfair and cruel things of this kind really happened in his time, though perhaps not in the concentrated and rapid sequences Voltaire depicts. At every turn in the plot, the philosopher Pangloss pops up to offer supposed "proofs" showing that what seems evil is really for the best in the end and everything is moving along as it should in the best of all possible worlds. The highly effective satire works by juxtaposing abstract dogma with painful reality. Pangloss and the Leibnizian optimism that he pontificates on every available and unsuitable occasion seem simply absurd.

"Evil" may strike us as a theological category, but theology does not offer an easy understanding of evil. Faith in a powerful God does not make pain and injustice disappear, and the challenge of understanding is placed within a framework of metaphysics and mystery. None of this proves, of course, that evil does not exist. The problem theologians face is grounded on the plain facts of human experience and human testimony. People do terrible things. Severe, unjustified pain and suffering do exist. To parrot Rabbi Kushner, bad things do happen to good people.

Leaving religion and theology aside, can we make sense of secular evil? At the risk of sounding hopelessly mundane, I have to confess that I personally understand evil acts as those that are severely morally wrong. By this I mean that they profoundly negate the intrinsic value of persons by imposing severe harm on them, with the implication that their most basic rights and most fundamental and serious human interests count for nothing and can simply be disregarded. From this secular point of view, evil acts are a subcategory of wrong acts: those that are markedly, extremely wrong, more than peccadilloes or ordinary misdeeds. In most contexts, for example, to knowingly make a promise one could not keep would be wrong but not evil. To make such a promise to a vulnerable and innocent person, knowing that the person was going to suffer terribly when one didn't keep the promise, would be wrong, severely wrong. One could call such an action evil. To foreseeably kill civilians when firebombing an enemy city would be wrong and arguably evil; to intentionally kill millions of civilians by herding them into gas chambers was certainly evil. To kill someone in a moment of rage would be wrong; to plot for years to kill thousands of people by turning a hijacked plane into a weapon of mass destruction would be evil.

Evil acts are sometimes committed. And evildoers are people who commit evil acts. If we ignore the distinction between the acts and the moral agents who commit these acts, we will be led to the conclusion that the terrorists and those who collaborated with them are evildoers. All who collude with terrorists everywhere are complicit with evil and are evildoers, just as President George W. Bush has said in his speeches.

I don't exactly dispute the starting point here. It really is evil to hijack planes and kill flight attendants with box cutters and fly the planes into tall buildings full of people. But I'm worried about some of the implications.

The problem is, so little is explained in this account. We seem to know only that extremely bad things are done and that people are out there, doing them or sponsoring them. And we call these people evil. But that's not exactly helpful because it doesn't tell us anything about their motives and the underlying causes of their having those motives, and the causes structuring the situation in which these acts were committed. If we grant that the perpetrators are evil, we should not stop there. We should go on to ask what we mean when we say this. What makes people evil? Is it that they lack empathy and sympathy, that they are cruel and place no value on the lives they are so willing to destroy? How many evil acts does a person have to commit to have an evil character? How permanent does an evil character have to be to make a person an evil person? If there are evil persons, are they barbarous and savage, primitively uncivilized? Or are they human beings potentially like us, but dupes of an ideology propagandized by charismatic leaders? Are they frustrated people lacking opportunities and a sense of meaning in their lives? Are they completely irredeemable? How does a person come to commit acts of evil? Is it because that person has no humane feelings? Or because he or she suppresses humane feelings? Or feels sympathy and empathy only for persons on the "right" side of a political conflict? Have evil persons no conscience? Or are their consciences deluded or distorted in some fundamental way?

Adolf Hitler was evil. He performed and authorized evil acts. Thus he had an evil character. So, too, did many of the people who supported him and carried out his orders. But does Hitler's evil character explain the Holocaust? Is the Holocaust best understood by saying "Well, Hitler was an evil character, and he had free will, so he chose to do all sorts of evil things, and that's how these 6 million people came to die"? That this won't work as an explanation is obvious; those events happened some sixty years ago and have been the subject of vast amounts of scholarly and imaginative reflection. Thousands of scholars have produced thousands of accounts seeking explanations of the Holocaust that appeal to cultural, economic, and political factors. Hitler was evil, and he planned and commanded many evil acts. Many will call him a moral monster, but doing that won't offer much understanding of the cooperation he received or the context of the German history and society that made all this possible. The same can be said about other agents of evil: Idi Amin, Saddam Hussein, Hutu advocates of genocide against the Tutsis, and Slobodan Milosevic, to name just a few. From the point of view of a secular morality in which human life is valuable and human suffering deplorable, we can call the actions of all these people evil. We may wish to go further and say that these people themselves are evil. The labels have a use because they help us express our repugnance and horror. But they don't help much when we come to explanation. To say "It's evil" announces a problem; it doesn't articulate a solution. It is a branding, a labeling, and a dangerously misleading one.

The problem is that the category of evil has such an absolutist ring to it. You have to be against evil, and who wouldn't be? In its dark magnitude, evil feels beyond our comprehension. We don't understand it; we couldn't understand it. And we wouldn't want to. A fundamental problem with "evil" and "evildoers" as explanatory concepts is that they function as thought stoppers.

Another danger in the rhetoric of evil is that this terminology is so starkly and permanently polarizing, so dangerously and absolutely Us versus Them. The notion of evil is so darkly harsh that we almost never accept its application to ourselves. To be sure, many among us are able to acknowledge having acted wrongly or unfairly on occasion. We may admit to having had conflicting impulses, having pursued our interests to the serious detriment of others, having made excuses and rationalizations for our moral failings. But we are unlikely to admit to evil: the label is too harsh and absolute for us to apply it to ourselves. Publicly, we share the responsibility for policies that buttress oppressive regimes, support financial institutions that bring appalling hardship to extremely poor people, damage the global environment to jeopardize future generations, or maintain a defense policy based on threatening to use nuclear weapons for our own security. Privately and publicly, we know ourselves to be complex beings acting in a complex world in which we have a great capacity to do harm. We show many tendencies and impulses, we make mistakes of judgment and even of value; we act wrongly. But because we are the people doing these things, or supporting them, we indulge ourselves in confident assumptions that we are not evil and what we do is not evil. Evil is categorically negative. And so we assume that it is always perpetrated by others. Never by us.

Suppose that evil exists. And suppose it is total, permanent, ineradicable, and an incomprehensible challenge to everything good. What are the implications? In a framework of absolutist thought, the most immediate and obvious answer is "destroy it." The evil of the Other is conceived as something beyond negotiation and reform. We cannot moderate it; there is no point in dialogue or negotiation; we would risk our own purity should we seek reconciliation or understanding. Logically, it should be possible to negotiate even with people who are evil (after all, they are human agents who might change); but psychologically and rhetorically, the idea that these are agents of evil will select a destructive and uncompromising response. We will eradicate it, destroy this evil thing wherever it is on the earth—and do whatever we need to do to get there.

Does Osama bin Laden possess nuclear weapons, or nuclear materials? Have bin Laden and members of his organization sought to obtain such materials? If so, from whom, and with what degree of success? What would they plan to do with those materials if they obtained them? What about bin Laden's statement that he had nuclear weapons and regarded them as a deterrent he would use only in response to a nuclear attack by the United States? How are such words best interpreted? Let us assume, with President Bush, that this man is evil. The problem is, this won't tell us what he wants, what he intends to do, and how he plans to go about it.

There are things to be said in defense of President Bush and his many references to evil. He is, after all, making public speeches at a time of crisis, not addressing a philosophy seminar at Harvard. And so, one might say, remarks about evil and evildoers really shouldn't be criticized. The circumstances made them appropriate. One might say that what President Bush said about evildoers was appropriate in the context of a war. Wartime leaders have no obligation to engage in subtle and complicated reasoning about their enemies; Winston Churchill made impassioned speeches and didn't stop to think about whether Hitler had endured a miserable childhood or how the Treaty of Versailles led to economic hardship and resentment and humiliation in Germany. He didn't give lectures at Oxford and seek to refute theories of Aryan supremacy by raising logically salient objections. The war was on; the point was to fight in the air and on the beaches, understand that They were evil and We were good, destroy Them, and win. War is no occasion for reflective analysis; in war you call a spade a spade and an evildoer an evildoer. And if somebody is an evildoer, you speak right up and say so and then you get your troops out there and you destroy the evildoer. That's what it's all about. Wars aren't subtle. It's us against them, and the goal is destruction. Evil is absolute; and they're evil. We're opposed to evil; we're the forces of good. What should the good do about evil? Eradicate it. Completely eliminate it from the earth.

I understand this defense, but I don't agree with it. The rhetoric of evil is dangerous. The epithet is too absolute to be helpful. It doesn't explain anything; it suggests complete polarization; it implies a need to destroy the enemy by whatever means we can. And—perhaps most dangerous of all—it will stop us from looking in the mirror.

4

HATRED

In September 2001, Irish Protestants in north Belfast screamed hatred at small girls being escorted by their mothers to the Catholic Holy Cross school, which lay in the Protestant community of Glenbryn. The girls, some as young as four, appeared tearful and terrified as they braved lines of jeering and spitting adults whose faces were distorted in grimaces of hatred. Pictures of these little girls and their mothers running a gauntlet of adult hatred simply to reach a primary school were so appalling that even hardened Protestant para-militaries were shocked. The dispute escalated until stones and bricks were thrown and even blast bombs were detonated. A school bus was stoned and an enraged Catholic motorist struck and killed a Protestant teenager; this death set the stage for further conflicts between the communities.

As individuals, these little Irish girls from the Catholic district of Ardoyne could not possibly have constituted a threat to adults in the Protestant community of Glenbryn. They were objects of hatred because they were Catholic children, and their walk to this school in this Protestant neighborhood represented the demographic reality that Catholics were beginning to outnumber Protestants in the area. To these people, and to many others, economic and political resources seemed finite. If there were more Catholics in north Belfast and Catholics received more than they previously had, then these Protestants—who thought they weren't doing very well anyway—would receive less.

As human beings, we sometimes hate each other individually. But much of our hatred is more generalized and directed toward groups. In Ireland, or in the Balkans, group hatred may be based on memories and resentments that have festered over decades or centuries. When we think the actions of individuals and small groups who threaten us represent the character and motives of larger groups, we tend to blame everyone in the larger group for what has gone wrong. We try to protect ourselves, striking back in anger—and we encourage other people to do that, too.

To outside observers, the display of group hatred in Belfast seemed appalling and absurd. The little girls looked so small and innocent, and the adults appeared so vicious and threatening. For foreign observers it seemed incredible. How could people feel so strongly and display their feelings so cruelly? The scene suggested a painful lesson about the power of hatred and its prominence in so many conflicts. In the Balkan wars of the 1990s, there were stories of atrocities committed against neighbors who had lived peacefully in common communities under Marshal Tito's Communist regime. People who had for years attended birthday and New Year's parties together were suddenly engaging in pillage, rape, and murder, all a result of ethnic animosities. Forty years of such coexistence wasn't enough to rule out vicious hatred when political leaders wanted to stir it up. The alarming scenario recalls *Nineteen Eighty-Four*, George Orwell's satire of hate. In a regularly scheduled "Two Minute Hate," people were led into "a hideous ecstasy of fear and vindictiveness, a desire to kill, to torture, to smash faces in with a sledge-hammer." It was a frenzy of rage, but abstract in a curious way, because "it could be switched from one object to another like the flame of a blowlamp." Orwell believed that hate was dangerous, and dangerously manipulable.

The nineteen hijackers of September 11 were all of Middle Eastern background; fifteen were citizens of Saudi Arabia. In the aftermath of these attacks, President George W. Bush was careful to avoid the implication that all Muslims, or all Arabs, shared responsibility for the hijackings. He even made a point of visiting a mosque. Nor did the president and other Western leaders incite hatred against Muslims, Arabs, or brown-skinned immigrants. Their restraint was good logic, because the attitudes and actions of nineteen individuals cannot reliably characterize those of millions. It was good citizenship, because millions of Americans are Arab or Muslim, and tens of millions have brown skin. And it was also good politics: the U.S. administration wanted support from Muslim countries in its campaign against terrorism.

Unfortunately, this caution did not prevent outbursts of hatred in the United States and other Western countries. Many fearful Americans spoke of "these people" after September 11, meaning brown-skinned immigrants. They viewed the attackers as brutal people who had taken advantage of a free and wealthy society only to turn against their hosts in a vicious attack. Months later, some were still saying that "these people" should not be allowed to remain in the country. One common expression of hostility demanded that Middle Easterners "go back where you came from and we'll bomb you." Mosques and temples were vandalized and some people were killed, including a Sikh in Arizona who was by no means a Muslim or an Arab. These responses of pain, rage, and fear categorized the hijackers as representatives of a much broader group of threatening and terrifying people. Governments did not incite hatred, but public expressions of it were all too real.

Clearly hatred was incited on the other side. The al Qaeda network and other fundamental Islamic movements are virulently anti-Western and still more virulently anti-American. Every American is seen as a degenerate enemy, a being who deserves to be robbed and killed. The destruction or humiliation of any American should be a source of triumph and delight. Descriptions of *madrassas* in northern Pakistan, where many members of the Taliban had been trained, tell of an "education" consisting only of rote study of the Koran, weapons training, and the inculcation of passionate anti-Americanism. In such schools Americans are portrayed as corrupt, greedy, irreligious, and evil; they are disrespectful of the holy Koran, they despise Islam, and they lack regard for the value of Muslim lives. The incited hatred lasts much longer than the two minutes satirized by Orwell; it continues, intensively, for years. Wealth and power in the United States are objects of enormous resentment; they are blamed for most of the ills of the world and all the ills of the Islamic world. The solution? Every able-bodied Muslim man who can possibly do so should make holy war against the United States. Hundreds of thousands of young Muslims hear this message and many apparently regard Osama bin Laden, a wealthy disseminator of it, as a heroic and courageous leader.

In 1997, Bin Laden said, "Mentioning the name of Clinton or that of the U.S. government provokes disgust and revulsion." In 1998, he urged all Muslims to kill Americans and steal their money, "anywhere, any time, and whenever possible."

Watching televised scenes of screaming crowds in northern Pakistan and elsewhere, I felt the virulent anti-Western hatred. I found it frightening to think that I represented corruption and decadence to these furious crowds. A newspaper story explained how liberated Western women were the most despicable representation of Western culture to these Muslim men: We were what they would have to tolerate if "their side" lost and "our side" won. They would no longer be automatically superior to half the human race. It was shocking and painful to imagine how intensely these enraged and screaming men resented my culture, my education, my freedom, and my gender. Me and everything I was. It seemed they could have torn me and everyone like me to pieces in an orgy of destructive fury. Even from the safe distance of my comfortable living room, I found it frightening to be the object of someone else's hatred. I felt lucky that these people were continents away, but fearful lest they come closer. When people experience hatred closer to home, in the communities in which they live, it must be terrifying.

There may be an evolutionary explanation for rage and hatred. Possibly such responses had a protective value and contributed to survival in primitive human societies. A follower of Charles Darwin might argue that the hatred of our enemies is a deeply natural thing, especially in a context where we have been attacked and believe that our survival is in question. I won't pretend to know how to apply the theory of evolution in this case. What I do know is that even if one assumes that hatred is in some sense natural, it doesn't follow that it's right or good. In our modern world, characterized by overcrowding, mixed populations, advanced technologies, and layers of complex interdependence, inciting hatred is downright dangerous.

Political hatred is a horrifying thing, but a search on the Internet suggests there are alarming amounts of it. A Racial Holy War page offers "Lyrics for a Declaration of War" against Jews, leftists, and nonwhites. It uses such expressions as "hook-nosed bastard," "nigger," "wild apes," and "mud race," warning that because "you're threatening the Welfare of my Race, your time is coming." An antigay site refers to homosexuals as "fags" and claims they prey on children, eat feces, and receive enemas as aspects of sexual pleasure. Vicious antifemale propaganda refers to women as "bitches" and "whores." Musician Eminem chants about how he savors raping and murdering his own mother—after all, she's a woman, too, and for him, just as despicable as all the others. If these things don't alarm you, you're probably not Jewish, brown, black, politically left-of-center, gay, or female. Even so, you may feel threatened by the anti-American and anti-Western hatred of radical Islamists.

A classic work by Jack Levin and Jack McDevitt distinguishes three kinds of hate crimes. There are those in which young punks are out for a thrill: a night of cross-burning or gay-bashing, or a gang rape in which they cry out against bitches and whores. There are responsive acts of hostility in which adult members of a community respond to what they regard as a personal threat against that community. That category includes the Protestants in Northern Ireland and the white citizens in the United States and other Western countries who hate brown-skinned immigrants. The third category is that of hate crimes of mission and applies to the September 11 terrorists and other perpetrators of anti-Western violence. In hate crimes of mission, people set forth to destroy persons or groups that they regard as diabolically evil. These evil forces are understood as threatening not only them and their community but ultimately the world itself. Hatred against the demonized enemy provides a meaning for otherwise frustrated lives: one can acquire status as a hero or martyr in a giant narrative of good and evil.

Frightened by the notion that I was an object of hatred, I became perversely interested in the topic when I came across Levin and McDevitt's book. These authors described how hostile and gross language, acts of symbolic vandalism, and brutal violence against randomly selected individuals make hatred deeply destructive to communities and societies. They sought understanding of hate crimes rather than hatred as a human emotion. The crimes they described were so destructive and offensive that moral conclusions about hatred seemed obvious. The problem of hatred as Levin and McDevitt understand it is not one of ethics or psychology. It's a matter of criminal offense, and the authors offered thoughtful suggestions about how to respond. Their extensive knowledge of the cruel and fearsome nature of hate crimes gave the impression that hatred is always something between groups, and is always objectionable. To these authors, the challenge of hate language and hate crimes wasn't exactly ethical. It was a problem in law and sociology.

I got a different impression when I began to discuss hatred in a local Philosophy Café. Fundamental philosophical questions soon emerged. Several men had a strong conviction that hate was a purely private feeling, natural to human beings and not properly a matter for legislative control. In their view, because hatred is an internal emotion, what we hate is our own business. It's not the business of any other person and it's no proper object of concern for legal authorities. If this account were correct, there would be no point in trying to understand hatred by offering a general definition of it or looking at expressions or actions inspired by hatred. Anyone who did that would be basically confused, because such an account would be mistaking expressions and actions for the private inner feeling, which is what hatred really is. Defenders of this idea that hatred is something private believed that we have our feelings because we're human beings—perhaps as a byproduct of our human evolution. And, or so the argument goes, we can know what goes on inside ourselves without consulting experts or looking words up in the dictionary. We are all familiar with that inner gut feeling we experience when we despise something, and that's what hatred is. It's not words of propaganda. It's not actions such as burning crosses on lawns, drawing swastikas on synagogues, chanting about bitches, or assaulting gays. Or bombing restaurants or hijacking planes. It's an inner sensation, part of our humanity—and as such, normal and acceptable.

The persistence of several men expressing this view in the Philosophy Café was striking and impressive in a way. It made me think. But their loud voices didn't convince me they were right. The debate recalled the elusive philosophy of Ludwig Wittgenstein who, in his later work, disputed the common assumption that emotions and feelings are purely private entities located in the mind or head and accessible only to the individual. Discussing the theory that pain is a private object unique to each person, Wittgenstein offered the analogy of a beetle in a box:

> Now suppose someone tells me that he knows what pain is only from his own case!—Suppose everyone had a box with something in it: we call it a "beetle." No one can look into anyone else's box and everyone says he knows what a beetle is only by looking at *his* beetle.—Here it would be quite possible for everyone to have something different in his box. One might even imagine such a thing constantly changing.

It's a strange image. What Wittgenstein was saying, I think, is that the word "beetle" couldn't refer to everybody's private, secret beetle, hidden somewhere in an obscure interior world, because then it would have no meaning. Words for feelings such as pain and hate function in public languages, and, Wittgenstein argued, they couldn't function in this way if they referred to solely private sensations. If the word "pain" did nothing but name a purely private sensation, it couldn't be a word in a public language. There would be nothing in the public observable world for it to refer to; thus there could be no rules to guide its use, and it could have no meaning. Wittgenstein argued that words in public languages such as English can't possibly derive their meanings from inner feelings alone. And he would surely have made this argument for "hate." We may have inner feelings of hate, but they can't be all there is because "hate" is a word in a public language. We express our hatred in gestures, words, and actions, and it's because we express our hatred in these ways that we can understand what hatred is.

Wittgenstein was prolific in his later years, but apparently he didn't write specifically about hatred. Thinking about the Philosophy Café, I found myself wishing he had. I thought his line of argument would apply aptly to the discussion. When we hate, we have feelings, to be sure. But hatred is not merely a feeling inside private consciousness that has nothing to do with other persons. Hatred of other persons is directed outward, against those other people. And that's the problem. If I had thought of all those jeering people in the streets of northern Pakistan as having private feelings in their heads, why would I feel afraid? Suppose each one has a private beetle in a box and all these beetles are undetectable by me. How could I be hurt? Why should I care? The problem is that the hatred of people is outward as well as inward. Intense hatred tends to culminate in degrading insults, destructive fury, and terrible crimes. In this instance I am one of those hated, and this makes me distinctly uncomfortable.

Hatred is an emotion of dislike and aversion; by definition, intense. (If our dislike for something is slight or moderate, we don't call it hatred or hate.) But to say that hatred is a feeling or emotion does not go far enough; hatred also involves expressions and actions and beliefs and moral evaluations. When we hate people, we conceive of them as having repugnant and despicable qualities that threaten us. Our emotions are founded on beliefs and those beliefs are about actions, events, and people in the public world. We articulate our beliefs by using public concepts and our own expressions, and what we say and do has an impact on the world we share with other human beings. Characteristically, people want to hurt or eliminate the objects of their hatred, and this is why hatred becomes a matter of public concern.

A philosopher friend told me emphatically that she hates injustice, and I said well, fine. I suggested there were lots of other abstract phenomena she might similarly hate: cruelty, brutality, and misogyny, for instance. Or evil. Or terrorism. Many people would say they hate such things, and it can be argued that everybody should. If hatred is the right attitude toward injustice, or evil, or terrorism, there may also be such a thing as righteous hatred; and I'll grant that righteous hatred is not morally objectionable. But these are side issues, I think. We don't have to conduct human relationships with abstractions such as injustice, misogyny, brutality, or terrorism. If we want to emphasize our aversion by saying we hate them, no harm is done. These are abstractions; their dignity and security will not be assaulted by hate; they aren't going to be damaged by words or acts of hateful violence. The real problem about hatred arises when other people become its objects.

The danger, I think, lies in thinking of particular individuals or groups as the embodiments of some abstraction we oppose. We have a tendency to project cruelty and evil onto other people. If we should hate injustice, should we hate people who are unjust? If we should hate terrorism, should we hate people who are terrorists? Or who aspire to become terrorists? (Call this personal hatred.) People who hate blacks or Jews or gays or women think they are monstrous and threatening and deserve to be hated. Radical Islamists who hate the United States and Americans believe that Americans are degenerate and dangerous and deserve to be hated. Could such hatred of human beings as individuals or groups ever be righteous? Could it be self-protective? Presumably those people who spat at schoolgirls in Northern Ireland thought it was. That's the problem. Alarm bells should be ringing at this point.

Hatred directed against such broadly defined groups is always objectionable. It's logically objectionable because relevant differences between people in the group are ignored. And this makes it morally objectionable as well: If we hate people simply because of their group membership, we are not treating those people as individuals. Hating *all* the members of a group because of the characteristics or actions of *some* of them amounts to stereotyping and bigotry. But what about the hatred of specific individuals who have committed particularly serious wrongs? Hitler, for instance? Or Osama bin Laden? Or more narrowly defined groups who incite acts of brutality or intend to commit them? Say, members of the Ku Klux Klan? What about the group "terrorists"? Or, still more specifically, "al Qaeda terrorists"? Wouldn't hatred be just the right attitude toward these people? Especially when we have solid evidence that they hate us, and want to destroy us?

Jeffrie Murphy once argued that hatred is the morally righteous attitude towards someone who has committed a serious wrong. He pointed out that our resentment of the wrongdoing can help us reassert our self-esteem, adding that a person who has committed a terrible wrong deserves to be hated because of what he has done. This argument is thought-provoking, but in the end, I disagree. The problem is that this thinking blurs the distinction between actions and agents. I'm uncomfortable with the suggestion that repeated wrongdoers may eventually be viewed as terminally "morally rotten." The act is not the agent; the sin is not the sinner; and even a wrongdoer should not be reduced to his wrongful acts. Even people who hate us, declare themselves our enemies, and commit awful violence against us remain human beings with human capacity for choice and change. If we make those people objects of our righteous hatred, we cut ourselves off from any prospect of a positive relationship with them.

It's a logical mistake to categorize all Muslims according to the evidence some of them present. And it's also a logical mistake to categorize a person, as an entire human being, based on the evidence of some of his actions. In the end, personal hatred implies a denial of the human capacities of people. No person—not even a terrorist—can be reduced to just one kind of thing.

Personal hatred is fearful and harmful to those people who are hated. But that's not all: It's also harmful to the people who hate. As Orwell suggested, personal hatred isn't good for us. We project intense energy in a negative direction. It's all too easy to disguise and avoid our own responsibility by blaming our problems on despised others. And that's not to mention the obvious political danger. If we cultivate hatred in ourselves, we're certain to inspire more of it in others.

Notes

An account of the events in North Belfast may be found in *Time* magazine for September 17, 2001. The phrases from George Orwell's *Nineteen Eighty-Four* are on pages 14—15 of the Penguin edition (Harmondsmith, U.K., 1954). Phrases from Osama bin Laden's statements are taken from Peter Bergen, *Holy War, Inc.: Inside the Secret World of Osama bin Laden* (New York: Free Press, 2001), 96, 100. The work by Jack Levin and Jack McDevitt is *Hate Crimes: The Rising Tide of Bigotry and Bloodshed* (1993; reprint, Boulder: Westview Press, 2001). Ludwig Wittgenstein's later philosophy is expressed in his *Philosophical Investigations*, trans. G. E. M. Anscombe (Oxford: Basil Blackwell, 1963). In chapter 10 of *Socrates' Children: Thinking and Knowing in the Western Tradition* (Peterborough, Ontario: Broadview Press, 1997), I offer a simplified account of Wittgenstein's ideas on emotions and states of mind. Jeffrie Murphy's ideas about moral hatred may be found in a book he co-authored with Jean Hampton, *Forgiveness and Mercy* (New York: Cambridge University Press), paperback edition 1990, and in his "Getting Even: The Role of the Victim," in Joel Feinberg and Jules Coleman, eds., *Philosophy of Law*, 6th ed. (Belmont, Calif: Wadsworth, 2000).

5

REVENGE

After the attacks on the United States, Americans felt not only vulnerable and afraid but humiliated and furious. Who were these men who could turn civilian flights into weapons of destruction? Who were these people sent forth as soldiers against a superpower and the civilized world to attack the most striking symbols of U.S. power? In addition to the enormous human, economic, and environmental damage, the attacks came as a blow to prestige and power. Shame and fury and a determination to get back at the enemy, to find those who did this and make them pay, were feelings shared by many. People couldn't be allowed to do such awful things with impunity.

When attacked, most people have an impulse to fight back, to hurt the enemy in turn and "get even," and the immediate rhetoric after September 11, 2001, was no exception to the pattern. When you seek revenge, you want to get even. You set out to hurt the party who hurt you and bring him down as much as he brought you down. He humiliated you by staging a damaging attack; by humiliating him in an equally damaging one, you want to prove that you're not one down. You prove his attack didn't put you down by showing that you've got the power and strength to put him down. Then you get the satisfaction of seeing him suffer at least as much as you have, and of knowing that you were the one who achieved this result. Here's a basic metaphor: before the fight start-ed, you and he were on a level. He attacked and hurt you; as a result of that first attack, your status went down and his went up. So, in response, you attack and hurt him. If you succeed, he goes down; and because you did it, you go up. The situation is restored to where it was before the attack. By striking back you've restored your status and position. Such is the logic of revenge. Respond to one wrong with another wrong, proportional to the first; respond to many wrongs with many more proportional ones. Through such moral arithmetic will the moral balance of the world be restored.

Revenge should be deeply rewarding because you get the satis-faction of hurting those who hurt you; the power you show in bringing this about will restore your self-esteem. That's one of the moral arguments in support of revenge. Another looks for justice between victims and perpetrators. It claims that when the victim strikes back successfully, the perpetrator gets what he deserves, and at that point, justice is done. Alternatively, one might contend that revenge is good because of its usefulness as a source of social soli-darity. When a group or nation is victimized, calling for revenge on the perpetrators is a quick and emotionally satisfying way to rally people to action. Then, too, there's the nonwimp argument, according to which you have to strike back to show your determi-nation and resolve. If you don't, people will think they can attack you again with impunity and you will look like a wimp. People who don't strike back in revenge are sending a message of powerless-ness. They are just going to sit there and take it—which couldn't possibly be the right thing to do. A revenge attack is simply retali-ation, and retaliation is entirely normal in violent conflicts. Furthermore, isn't revenge protective, a necessary step towards pre-venting future attacks?

Now none of this is Christian morality, that's clear. Didn't Jesus tell us to love our enemies? To turn the other cheek? Christian reli-gious institutions have rationalized plenty of violence in the name of Just War Theory, but Jesus seems to have adopted a more pacifist approach. He preached peace, forgiveness, and nonviolence; he did not preach revenge. Friedrich Nietzsche, by contrast, criticized the Christian morality of nonviolence and forgiveness as entirely too servile. When people hurt you, they make you suffer in ways you don't deserve. The natural human thing is to be angry about it and strike back in return. The Christian teaching that people should suppress such instincts will only turn them into cowards, Nietzsche said. Your feelings of rage and resentment are normal and real and shouldn't be suppressed. In fact, you should go right ahead and act on them. Fight back and do it vigorously; don't tell yourself to be patient and humble. Don't turn the other cheek; that just shows you have no pride. Strike right back at his cheek. And strike hard.

I'm surely no disciple of Nietzsche. But I'll admit to having sought revenge and sometimes feeling satisfaction when I thought I had managed to "get even." The contexts were modest; they didn't involve murder and mayhem. (I've been lucky enough to lead a relatively quiet life.) Still, there have been moments when I thought I had some conception of what the satisfactions of revenge might mean. But even in my relatively undramatic circumstances, I've found that one nasty act inspires further nasty acts in retaliation. It's been my experience that the satisfactions of revenge are fleeting, but the resulting animosities last a long time and are hard to overcome.

This brings me to the arguments against revenge.

Let's begin with the matter of satisfaction. The problem isn't only that this satisfaction is short-lived, if it exists at all. It's more basic; it concerns the moral credentials of the feeling. The satisfactions of revenge arise from the notion that our suffering and humiliation can be soothed by our delight in the suffering of our enemies, which is something we have brought about by our own actions. Immanuel Kant, for one, argued sternly against such notions. He believed it is despicable and malevolent to take satisfaction in bringing suffering to others. This kind of pleasure, Kant argued, is morally unworthy of us as human beings. To cultivate and indulge vindictive sentiments in ourselves is to cultivate a hatred of others and is contrary to every duty of humanity. In seeking revenge, we are cultivating in ourselves hatred and malevolence and making ourselves into agents of immorality. These sentiments are morally objectionable; they amount to violations of our duties to other people. And in cultivating malevolent desires in ourselves, we are making ourselves into worse people, which is fundamentally objectionable.

There's a more practical argument too. Often the satisfactions of revenge are only anticipated and never achieved. Jean Hampton used Hegel's philosophy to make this practical claim about revenge. Hegel theorized about the human need for recognition, which he claimed was so powerful that human beings seek acknowledgment from others even in circumstances of superiority where, in principle, they are so dominant that they shouldn't need it at all. Hegel's dialectic of the Master and the Slave tells a story about a frustrated quest for recognition. Suppose there were a Master who had a human relationship with only one other person, that person being his Slave. Needing recognition and acknowledgment, the Master would seek it from his Slave. But because of the underlying inequality between them, his quest would be doomed. The Slave is too humble to have the status to recognize the Master. And because he is in the power of the Master, he lacks choice about what he says and does. Any recognition he gives is unfree, and likely insincere. Under these circumstances of fundamental inequality, the Master can have no assurance that the deference of his Slave amounts to recognition. So it's a doomed dialectic. Hampton suggests that revenge scenarios bear a striking similarity to Hegel's tale of the Master and Slave. The victim seeks to reassert himself, to get over his humiliation and buttress his self-esteem by injuring or humiliating the perpetrator. But how will this work? A perpetrator brought low will be a humble and vulnerable human being, so much so that it will be impossible to take pride in conquering such a person. If a Taliban solider were hunched in fear, if an al-Qaeda member were shaved and held in shackles, the victims who had sought revenge would expect to find such humiliation satisfying. But these humiliated people are now vulnerable and desperate; they have been brought so low that it makes no sense to think that their suffering could compensate for the agonies of American victims. Even if bin Laden were captured, there might be a sense of frustrated anticlimax. In captivity, the man would likely seem frail, even impotent.

Quite apart from questions about the satisfactions of revenge, there's a more fundamental moral problem. It's this: getting even with one set of wrongs requires committing in response another set, acts that are equally wrong, or worse. The old adage "Two wrongs don't make a right" applies here. If it's wrong to do something once, it's wrong to do it twice. If victims commit wrongs to get even with perpetrators, they in turn become perpetrators. In all likelihood, victims will protest their innocence on the grounds that they were injured first, a rhetoric that recalls playground disputes and the protest that "he hit me first." The notion that we are innocent victims entitled to take revenge against those who attacked us before we attacked them is powerful and, to many, irresistible. But the point remains that no matter who hit first—or second or third—the avenging people will be committing wrongs just as severe as those they experienced themselves. If they didn't do that, they wouldn't be getting *even*. People who defend acts of revenge claim that when a victim gets even with the perpetrator, a moral balance is restored. But I don't find the defense plausible. If a "balance" is achieved by the reaction, it is established at the wrong level. If it's wrong for perpetrators to kill innocent American civilians, that's because killing innocent civilians is wrong. And if killing innocent civilians is wrong, wouldn't killing innocent Afghan civilians be wrong, by the same argument? If victims become perpetrators, any notion that moral progress has been made is illusory.

Then there's the practical argument against revenge, summed up elegantly in Mohandas Gandhi's comment that "with an eye for an eye, all the world will be blind." Attack and counterattack produce cycles of violence. The arguments for revenge, based on the need not to be a wimp, assert that we have to take revenge to prove our strength and determination and show that we can't be attacked with impunity. It's all supposed to end with the heroic response that will forever prove to the evildoers that we are right and they were wrong. But things rarely stop at stage two. Most revenge attacks provoke further attacks, which then inspire further revenge attacks, leading to an ongoing cycle of violence. You don't have to be especially wise or learned to detect this pattern. It isn't necessary to study blood feuds in Montenegro or recall the saga of the Hatfields and the McCoys. Any news broadcast of relations between the Israelis and the Palestinians will provide a horrendous illustration: a bombing, a suicide terrorist, an army reprisal, a funeral expressing rage, hate, and determination; the next bombing by terrorists, an army occupation of a village, more funerals, and so on. At every stage, bereaved women wail and orphaned children look on in bewilderment. And so it goes, again and again.

In Kosovo before 1999, Serbs were oppressing Kosovan Muslims and rationalizing their actions by appealing to the Battle of Kosovo in 1349 and the oppression of Serbs by Muslims under the Ottoman Empire. The Serbs saw themselves as a victimized people getting revenge against their oppressors. In the spring of 1999, NATO forces bombed Serbia, Serbian oppression in Kosovo escalated, and hundreds of thousands of Kosovans fled their province. I saved a cartoon that expressed the warning, "You can't bomb hatred." But under U.S. leadership, NATO forces did bomb Serbia and Kosovo. NATO proclaimed victory and said the bombing campaign had worked. In its aftermath, Albanian Kosovans returned to their homes. When I attended an information session on postwar peacekeeping some six months after the campaign, I was told that 50,000 representatives of the international community were at work trying to create civil order and a multiethnic society in Kosovo. Revenge attacks were a huge problem at this point. Kosovan Muslims who saw themselves as victims of Serb perpetrators were so enraged and threatening that most Serbs left the province of Kosovo; those who remained had to be protected by international personnel. One aid worker described how she helped arrange for Serb and Gypsy women to be escorted when they went shopping. NATO claimed success, but the result in Kosovo was far from a sustainable peace.

The practical problem with revenge is that you are likely to provoke attacks, not prevent them.

A rejoinder could point out that the war against terrorism is a special case in this respect, so special, in fact, that anxieties about the cycle of violence do not apply here. One might contend that, well, this campaign is going to be an exception: the perpetrators will simply be destroyed and there won't be a cycle of violence and counterviolence because there won't be anybody left on the perpetrator side. The idea is to remove the Taliban regime so that they can no longer play host to al-Qaeda; to kill or capture Taliban and al-Qaeda soldiers; and to deny al-Qaeda its access to territory and weapons. Eventually, to wipe out this network. The perpetrators will be devastated by all this; indeed, they will be eliminated, so they won't be able to attack again. And we won't have a situation like that of the Israelis and Palestinians, or of the Serbs and Albanians. We will have destroyed the evil empire of the terrorist al-Qaeda. No cycles of revenge need be feared. The story will end right there.

Revising my theories would be a small price to pay for such a feeling of security. I'd rather be safe than right; it would be such a comforting conclusion to think that the forces of anti-Western hatred had been defeated once and for all. As evidence shows, and as the U.S. administration admits, networks of terrorism in the name of radical Islam extend far beyond Afghanistan to Egypt, Pakistan, the Philippines, Saudi Arabia, Indonesia, and the Sudan. Sixty countries, it's said, including the United Kingdom, Germany, France, Spain, Canada, and the United States itself. It seems unlikely that destroying camps in Afghanistan could eliminate the capacity for retaliation and revenge on the other side. Nor is hatred of the United States and the West likely disappear if terrorists in Afghanistan and many other Muslim people are killed. If one resented the power of the United States before all this, would one's resentment disappear or diminish? It seems awfully unlikely. I can't help feeling that the cartoon was right: "You can't bomb hatred."

On November 12, 2001, American Airlines flight 587 went down in New York. This crash occurred just as troops of the Northern Alliance were approaching Kabul and the Taliban forces were in big trouble. More fire, more death. Alarmed, I switched on my television to find out what people were saying. I was reassured to hear that official sources regarded the event as a tragic accident, not the work of terrorists. Coverage switched to the White House. To my surprise, who should appear first on the screen but former South African president Nelson Mandela, standing with President George W. Bush in front of the White House. Mandela, Nobel Prize winner, great moral leader, spokesman for forgiveness in politics and cherished the world over for his imaginative leadership away from animosity and towards reconciliation. This was the man who spent twenty-seven years in prison and inspired the world when he emerged, without bitterness, to preach cooperation and national reconciliation to all South Africans. Father of the Rainbow Nation, postapartheid South Africa. Self-deprecatingly, Mandela often jokes that he's "a pensioner." But after leading his country on a path to reconciliation, he's still working for peace; in Burundi he's playing a lead role, urging Hutus not to take revenge against Tutsis, and hoping to avoid a bloodbath.

After the crash of American Airlines 587, Nelson Mandela and George W. Bush both expressed grief, sympathy for the victims of the crash, and dismay that people in New York were experiencing this tragedy so soon after the September 11 attacks. President Bush explained that Mandela was in Washington because of his role in Burundi and went on to praise his efforts there. The two men evidently agreed that another round of revenge killings in Burundi would not be a good thing. For me, the most fascinating aspect of this duo appearance was Mandela's comment on the military campaign in Afghanistan. He supported it strongly, urging Americans not to hold back, even if other people criticized them. They should continue to fight with all their might. To support his argument that the antiterrorist campaign should never falter, Mandela pointed to the thousands of victims on September 11. Bush reassured him: Americans weren't going to go soft on terrorism. There was nothing to worry about on that score.

Perhaps Mandela thought that the campaign in Afghanistan would be unique, that terrorist camps could be destroyed by military methods without contributing to a cycle of violence. Or perhaps he thought the bombing campaign had nothing to do with revenge and retaliation; it was not a context where mercy or forgiveness would be relevant, but rather something else. Self-defense or preemptive self-defense, perhaps. In any event, he seemed to think it would work.

I've admired this man for years and I wish I believed him in this case. But I don't.

Notes

Kant's comments on revenge can be found in his *Lectures on Ethics,* ed. and trans. Peter Heath (Cambridge: Cambridge University Press, 1993), 412, and can best be understood as expressing his idea that ethics is based on a consistent respect for all persons. The idea of thinking about revenge according to Hegel's Master/Slave dialectic was put forward by Jean Hampton in *Forgiveness and Mercy*, coauthored by Hampton and Jeffrie Murphy (New York: Cambridge University Press, 1988). Bush and Mandela appeared together on a broadcast on the Canadian Broadcasting Corporations's *Newsworld* at 11 A.M. (Mountain Standard Time) on November 12, 2001. Several later versions of the presidential statement had edited Mandela out and showed only President Bush.

As of January 2004, Osama bin Laden had still not been captured, although it was generally agreed that he was still alive.

After the defeat of his regime in Iraq, Saddam Hussein was dramatically captured in December 2003. That case is more available, so far as the humiliation of the enemy and the satisfactions of revenge are concerned. Saddam Hussein had been hiding out in what was literally a hole in the ground. He was found in a disoriented and disheveled condition and submitted to a physical examination by his captures, which included a widely televised probe into his mouth. In the media, much was made of this capture. An important issue was that of humiliation. Was the humiliation of Saddam Hussein a good thing, because it demonstrated his definitive defeat? Or was it, by contrast, politically hazardous as a spur to further anti-American terrorism? (There is good evidence that feeling humiliated, as an individual or group, is a prime cause of resorting to violence as a means of self-assertion.) Within a few weeks of his capture, the topic of 'Saddam' mysteriously disappeared from the news and there was no word as where the captured dictator was being kept or what was happening to him.

6

POWER

Thomas Hobbes is the great philosopher of power. There is in man "a perpetuall and restlesse desire of Power after power, that ceaseth onely in Death," Hobbes said, writing in a seventeenth-century England that had been torn by civil war. His words echo poignantly today. According to Hobbes, power is the most fundamental of all human desires. He defined power as our ability to get what we want—servants, friends, riches, or a reputation—and most of all, more power. We crave power not so much because our desires are infinite (more, more, more) but because we are afraid of losing what we already have. Our restless longing for power is founded on fear and insecurity.

Even the strong are not secure, Hobbes warned, for the weak could form alliances and kill the strong "either by secret machination, or by confederacy with others." Without a reliable central authority, all are in danger, in a condition of "warre; and such a warre, as is of every man against every man." Foul weather is not a matter of a shower or two, but a tendency to clouds and showers over some days; and similarly, war is not just a matter of fights and battles, but the standing possibility that these may occur. The insecurity that arises from the human lust for power will make life "solitary, poore, nasty, brutish, and short." There is only one solution, Hobbes argued: an all-powerful Sovereign authority.

Interestingly, the philosopher of power also had a lot to say about moral authority and relationships. He thought it would be a misunderstanding to think of power as some kind of entity that we could possess or fail to possess; power can't be understood by considering persons or institutions in isolation. We have power only in relation to other people: one person is powerful because another person is willing to defer to him. Hobbes thought that power requires deference, which means that consent is based on some reason. In the end, he says, power is based on honor and obedience. Even dueling fits the theory; a man will only gain credibility from conquests in duels if the duel is a respected institution. So brute physical power is not as brute as it looks: it is ultimately founded on reputation and respect, or what we might today call public opinion. Ultimately, a person can have power only if other people are prepared to defer to him or her. And the same can be said of a nation state.

Mohandas Gandhi also wrote about power, and there is a surprising degree of agreement between him and Hobbes. Although Gandhi was a theorist of nonviolence, he is like Hobbes in the way he relates power to deference. Writing in 1905, Gandhi argued that it would be impossible for the British to rule India by physical coercion alone. Hundreds of men cannot, by themselves, suppress millions of people; to suppose that they could would be to believe in a physical impossibility. The British ruled because enough Indian people cooperated to make their rule possible. In effect, Gandhi argued, the Indians deferred to imperial rule; withdraw their consent and British power would disappear. Such withdrawal wouldn't require violence on the part of the resisters, Gandhi argued; physical power was based on obedience, which could be nonviolently withheld. What was needed for Indian independence was the withholding of consent.

Some seventy years later, Vaclav Havel took a similar stance. Havel wrote about "the power of the powerless" in Communist-dominated eastern Central Europe. His point was that ordinary people who thought of themselves only as oppressed were colluding to make these regimes possible. They regarded themselves as blameless, but they weren't blameless because they weren't powerless. Rather, they had a kind of power that had gone largely unnoticed. For all the grumbling and discontent, in effect their consent had been obtained by the authorities. Consent was required to make the regimes work; if it were withdrawn, tanks and guns wouldn't be enough to maintain them.

In early December 1989, the Romanian dictator Nicolae Ceausescu appeared to be securely in charge of his country. Despite a few occasions of unruly rebellion, he had long ruled by bizarre decree and was expected to do so indefinitely. Ceausescu gave a lengthy speech to a vast room full of party supporters who applauded with stolid enthusiasm. Secure with this support, he gave another speech a week later, this time in front of a huge crowd in downtown Bucharest. At first the response was as expected, with people yelling "Ceausescu si popurul." Then a single voice called out, "Ceausescu dictatorul." The entire crowd began to yell against the repressive leader, and the mood changed in a single moment. Ceausescu's face crumbled and his demeanor of confidence gave way to an image of craven fear. In a televised instant he had become a small vulnerable man facing thousands of furious people. The consent for his authority had disappeared; his power had gone. It was the beginning of the end for this dictator, who was executed a week later. Gandhi's ideas—and Hobbes'—were apparently confirmed.

Military power exists in missiles, bombs, tanks, and guns. With military power, a nation can launch missiles at airports, bomb communications equipment, wreck transportation routes, and kill enemy soldiers. It can physically destroy enemy resources and enemy people—and, in the nuclear age, the world itself. If the meaning of power is understood as the capacity to destroy, every nation possessing nuclear weapons is a powerful nation and the United States is the most powerful of them all.

But power is not fundamentally about destructive capacity, and the human desire for power is not at root a desire to destroy as many things as possible. Or even to be able to destroy them in the name of something else, such as self-defense or national security. The quest for power is a quest for the security of life and possessions. That's not to say that the notion of military security is a mere misnomer. Obviously, nations build up weapons and alliances in the name of security, and people generally support that approach because they want security and personal safety. That kind of security is what so many of us fear we lost on September 11, and we would like to restore it. Modern military equipment tends to be intricately computerized, high-tech, glitzy, and expensive; for some, it has an enticing metallic glamor. But it encourages misunderstandings: All the hardware tempts us again to think of power as things and to forget that power is not a thing at all, but an aspect of relationships. Even nuclear weapons do not represent power pure and simple. A nation could use them to destroy everything, but short of that, coercive use involves people and their attitudes. If you are going to wield influence by making a nuclear threat, somebody somewhere will have to find it credible and give in.

Of course, no strategic analyst ever literally believed that power lay in a weapon or a fortification alone. Military capacity is supposed to supply coercive force, but most of the time this doesn't mean actually attacking anybody. You don't have to use your weapons to go out and smash things and kill people. Instead, you can let your military resources serve as a kind of standing, unexpressed threat to indicate without saying anything that people should do what you want—or else. If the implied threat is insufficient, you can make an explicit threat. Or something in between—as when the United States said in October 2001 that it could not guarantee that it would not use nuclear weapons in

Afghanistan. The idea of military resources as tools of coercion is that the other should be intimidated, give in, and come within your orbit of control.

A nation can use its military resources to threaten destruction in efforts to compel cooperation and obedience. The problem is, it's harder to achieve control than to achieve destruction: eventually we arrive again at the awkward reality that on the other end of our weapons there exist human beings whom we need to persuade to consent to our exercise of authority.

As the damage from wars becomes more apparent, we can only think the whole activity is desperately bad for the environment and all sensitive creatures. It seems such a crude instrument, military force. And in addition, it's wildly expensive. And costly in another sense too: A nation that uses it too much is likely to get an unpleasant reputation for throwing its weight around.

Naturally, the United States sought to destroy terrorist camps in Afghanistan and unseat the Taliban regime that had harbored and supported al-Qaeda. Lots of bombs and missiles were employed, and together with the efforts of Northern Alliance troops on the ground, military force seemed to do the trick. An article in the *New York Times* proclaimed, "Surprise. War Works After All," and in a sense, it had. But even in this case, the Taliban collapse was not entirely a matter of military force. By mid-November, many Afghan people who did not like the harsh Taliban regime had risen up against it. Sensing their unpopularity in these altered circumstances, the Taliban fled some key centers without much fighting. After appearing relatively solid only weeks before, the regime suddenly seemed to dissolve. Much of its political support had been as unreal as Ceausescu's.

At this point, newspapers and journals began to run stories about contending non-Taliban factions in Afghanistan and the difficulties of negotiating for reconstruction. How would the United States and its coalition partners be involved? There was talk of sending troops to make roads safe enough to deliver humanitarian aid. Then, it seemed, the situation was too unstable even for those efforts, and troop departures were delayed. There was chaos "on the ground," and things were happening so fast that Western powers and the United Nations couldn't keep up. Persuading contending powers to work together to reconstruct the country was going to be a complicated matter. Essential to any new order was assurance that Western security would not be further threatened by terrorist activities based in Afghanistan. Given this fundamental interest, along with the survival of thousands of Taliban soldiers and the need to include contending factions and ethnic groups, the problem of somehow constructing a viable democratic society in this devastated country was enormous. For that task, destruction and threats to destroy would not be enough.

This naturally brings us to another theme, that of economic power. The idea that power is not a thing but an aspect of relationships between people applies here too. We can begin by thinking of economic power simply as the ability to command money and move it around; those who can do this can thereby persuade others to defer to them by offering money or goods, or by threatening loss. A nation possessing economic power can motivate people to cooperate with its plans because it has resources that other people want.

The dollar is sometimes said to be all-mighty, but in the end, money isn't the real basis of economic power. It's a stand-in for other things: resources, products, productivity, entrepreneurship, innovation, trade potential. And, by no means incidentally, confidence. Dollars are a medium of exchange and, like any currency, they can serve their role today only if people believe they will be able to use them to obtain goods and services tomorrow. The so-called all-mightiness of the dollar depends on something inchoate and ephemeral: the confidence of the human beings who are going to use it.

All this bears on the problem of sustainable peace in Afghanistan. Consistent with the idea that power depends on acceptance, and greatly relevant in the context of efforts to build peace, is the use of economic power to threaten or to entice. There's the stiff economic stick (unlike the military stick, a metaphorical one) and the bright economic carrot.

In the spring of 1999, NATO used its military power to bomb Serbia. The bombing lasted for seventy-eight days, produced massive destruction in Serbia and Kosovo, and took the lives of at least six hundred civilian Serbs. Some 800,000 Albanian Kosovans fled their province, most of them after the bombing had begun, because at that point Serb fury exposed them to terrible harm. This military effort is said to have cost some $5 billion, and that doesn't include the costs of rebuilding when the violence ended and most of the Albanian Kosovans returned. The idea underlying the military campaign was to compel the Milosevic regime to withdraw Serb forces from Kosovo, thereby ending Serbian control of the province and human rights violations by Serbs in that area. When Serbia capitulated to some key demands by the United States and its NATO allies—including provisions for a referendum on Kosovan independence after several years—NATO pronounced its military campaign a success. Most Western commentators agreed. Interestingly, though, it wasn't the bombing that brought Milosevic to the war crimes tribunal in The Hague. A key element of that story was the plump carrot of economic assistance—the granting by the United States of a generous aid and reconstruction package to a more democratic Serbia following Milosovic's electoral defeat in the fall of 2000. After more than a decade of bitter Balkan wars, the Serbian people wanted to start afresh and end their isolation from the rest of the world. Doubts notwithstanding, the new leaders wanted U.S. economic assistance so much that they were willing to turn Milosevic over to the tribunal. So they gave in.

Thinking about all this, I don't really find evidence to refute the basic idea put forward by Hobbes and Gandhi. It seems that for Serbia, too, power involved deference and consent. Whether it's Romania or the Czech Republic, Kosovo or Afghanistan, the point seems to remain. You can exert control and influence only with the consent of other people, although you don't need their consent to destroy them or their property. If you threaten them, they have to fear what you are threatening and choose to avoid it by doing what you want. And if you offer them something as an enticement, they have to want that thing enough to cooperate in return for it. Resistance is possible. As Gandhi would say, these other people can deny their consent. As Hobbes would put it, they can choose not to defer to your demands and requests; they can deny you the honor of obeying.

Which is just to say the same thing all over again. Given that the United States and its allies want more than destruction in their struggle against terrorism, power is going to come down to fundamental matters of relationships. The United States and its allies in the coalition against terror want security and enough control over territory and actual and potential terrorist enemies to provide for that security. This means that Western nations are going to need a lot of power, which we will try to obtain by employing military and economic resources. But even more intractable than the problem of reconstruction in Afghanistan is this huge and vague and highly recalcitrant reality that millions of people dissent from Western values and styles and resent U.S. wealth and military power. They may not willingly grant the deference needed for us to exercise our power and enjoy security.

In the fall of 2001, Tom Naylor, a scholar of international crime and money laundering, was asked to comment on efforts to deny terrorists their financial backing. He said he approved of the efforts, but didn't think money was the terrorists' most important asset. In his opinion, "the key resource is *determination,*" which is something "you can't freeze in a bank account." The remark points back to convictions based on values.

We might think of power as influence instead of coercion, and that conception more readily suggests a relationship with some authority at each end. Obviously, a nation can exert influence because of its military and economic power, which explains much of the power of the United States. But this is the merest beginning because it omits cultural power. Television, movies, fashion, food, language. Scholarship, knowledge, science, medicine, technology. Business practices. Newspapers, literature, art. The United States exerts enormous influence for many reasons: its pluralism, its open institutions, its brash, vibrant culture, its efficiency and energy, and its capacity to change. Millions—arguably, billions—of people choose to purchase or emulate American styles and artifacts. The United States has great cultural power. Applauded by many, decried by many others, for better or for worse, that cultural power is a reality of our world. At some level, those who consume or support American culture could say no. Influence depends on the consent of those influenced. Mostly, people around the world do consent, and as a result the cultural power of the United States is vast indeed. This, too, is part of the story of power.

People consent for various reasons. Sometimes they consent because there is an explicit or implicit threat of destruction or harm. Sometimes they consent because they are attracted by something. All this may seem to be the push and pull of human desire. The phenomena may suggest that we could manipulate people to get the cooperation we need. It might seem that consent has little to do with reasoning, or values, or what's sometimes called legitimacy. You threaten something people are afraid of or offer them something they want; then, as a result of your efforts, they do what you want. If you possess the resources to do that, the power is yours to wield, the security yours to buy—or so you may think. Sometimes your influence is positively attractive; when it isn't, you can manipulate consent. That may involve entering into a propaganda war in which your task is to win.

So the argument might go like this. Even granting the various subtleties and dimensions of power, and even granting that power presupposes consent, if you have the resources to coerce or manipulate people, you can do it and get the power you need for your own security. Realpolitik on the weapons level, the all-mighty dollar, and the manipulation of public opinion: Now put all this together and you're really talking. In the end, coercive and manipulative apparatus will do the trick. Nothing like "informed consent" or the "reasonable consent" is required, apparently, and only naïve idealists would look for reason and moral authority in all this.

I don't think so. And it's not only my philosophical biases that make me doubt it. It's not just ethics and logic, and my readings of Immanuel Kant on the necessary independence and transparency of public reason. It's my conviction that, in the end, moral authority cannot be neglected. I would argue that it's the core of the matter. Propaganda, manipulation, and coercion exist in this world, and in vast amounts, but they won't suffice in the end. Legitimacy is what's needed, and for just the reasons Hobbes, Gandhi, and Havel explained. Fundamentally, moral authority requires that you have something worth defending and are convinced for good reasons that it is worth defending. And you can justify your values and attitudes to the other people whose cooperation you want and need. All this requires a shift from military defense to defense by reason, evidence, and argument.

I'd appeal here to Abraham Lincoln's famous statement, "You can fool all the people some of the time and some of the people all the time, but you cannot fool all the people all the time." Substitute "coerce" for "fool," and I think Lincoln's statement still applies. Eventually, some of the people, or all of them, will resent the stiff stick of coercion and even some of the rosy carrots of enticement.

They will see through manipulations and resist by withdrawing their cooperation—and the power needed to ensure our security will dissipate. To defend ourselves and establish sustainable relationships with other people, we have to know what we're defending and why. There's no way around it.

Notes

Quotations from Thomas Hobbes are from the *Leviathan,* introduced by C. B. Macpherson, ed. (Middlesex, England: Penguin Books, 1968), first published 1651. Gandhi's ideas are explained in Gene Sharp, *Gandhi as a Political Strategist* (Boston: Sargent, 1979). Havel's essay, "The Power of the Powerless," may be found in his collection *Living in Truth,* trans. Paul Wilson (London: Faber and Faber, 1986). The changes in Romania in 1989 were described by Pavel Campeanu in "The Revolt of the Romanians," *New York Review of Books,* February 1, 1990, 30–31. The *New York Times* article saying that war works appeared on November 18, 2001. Accounts of money and confidence can be found in Herbert S. Frankl, *Money: Two Philosophics: The Conflict of Trust and Authority* (Oxford: Basil Blackwell, 1977), and Niklas Luhmann, *Trust and Power,* trans. H. Davies, J. F. Raffman, and Kathryn Rooney (London: John Wiley and Sons, 1979). Milosevic was handed over to authorities in The Hague on April 1, 2001. A partial account of military and economic power in Serbia may be found in "Serbia's Struggle for Freedom," which was an edited version of a speech by Gene Sharp, as published in *Peace Magazine* (October–December 2001): 18–20. Sharp, a prominent theorist of nonviolent power, argues that neither tanks nor dollars ultimately defeated the Milosevic regime; rather, it was nonviolent opposition under principles proposed by Gandhi and developed by Sharp himself. Tom Naylor's remark about determination was quoted in Paul Knox, "The Money Weapon," *Globe and Mail,* November 16, 2001. According to the *Oxford Dictionary of Quotations,* Abraham Lincoln's statement was made in a speech on September 8, 1858.

The claim that military defeat requires a kind of power different from that needed for post-war reconstruction has been amply corroborated by difficulties in Afghanistan and, even more conspicuously, Iraq.

7

JUSTICE

In the wake of the September 11 attacks on the United States, President George W. Bush appealed repeatedly to the concept of justice, assuring his listeners that al-Qaeda terrorists and those who sponsor them would be brought to justice. One prominent occasion was an address at a military academy on November 21. At that point, thousands of Arab Afghans were trapped with Taliban forces in Khandahar and Kundez. What would happen to these people, who had traveled from their homes in Saudi Arabia, Indonesia, Egypt, and other countries to fight with the Taliban, often after training in al-Qaeda's terrorist camps? For that matter, what would happen to bin Laden himself, if he were caught? Bush assured his audiences that the wrongdoers would be brought to justice. Every single one.

Justice makes good rhetoric. Whatever justice is, everybody is in favor of it. Nobody is going to come out and say, "Well, I don't want them brought to justice."

Nevertheless, deep questions lurk beneath the rhetoric.

Long dear to philosophers, the concept of justice has been the subject of reflections and debates that echo through thousands of years. Even a cursory survey of recent writing suggests the many forms and contexts of justice. There's social justice, which concerns equity in matters of welfare, health policy, and opportunities. And, closely related, distributive justice, which deals with economic resources, who is entitled to them, and why. These were the major themes of John Rawls' prominent work, *A Theory of Justice*, which appeared in 1971. Rawls sought to understand justice through the justifiability and fairness of basic social institutions. He used a kind of social contract model to introduce the beautiful idea of an original position from which people would reason together about basic principles for social institutions before they knew what their own abilities, resources, or affiliations would be in society. Thinking in terms of the original position, you imagine yourself having to choose fundamental principles of justice in circumstances when you don't know your wealth, religious beliefs, abilities, or position in society. According to Rawls, it's as if you were reasoning from behind a "veil of ignorance." The principles of justice should not favor either rich or poor; abled or disabled; men or women; Christians or Muslims or Jews; atheists or believers. The fundamental idea was that within a society, just institutions should be fair to all its members.

Penal justice has to do with policies and principles governing the punishment of wrongdoers. In Rawls' account, the topic of punishment was a subtheme. Penal justice concerns who suffers which punishment, and why persons should receive punishment in the first place. The justice of punishment is often understood as retributive: This is the "eye for an eye" idea, according to which those who have committed wrong deserve to suffer for it in some manner proportionate to the seriousness of their offenses. Retribution is not the only basis for a theory of punishment, though. Punishment can also be understood in terms of crime prevention, rehabilitation, moral education, and restitution. Based on the belief that wrongdoers should make amends to victims, restitution lies at the core of what has come to be known as restorative justice. On this model, the best response to wrongdoing is not to impose penalties on wrongdoers but to have them make amends to victims in an effort to restore or construct decent relationships.

There are many rooms and corridors in the palace of justice. In addition to social, distributive, and penal justice, there's the justice of recognition, which concerns the legitimacy of demands for acknowledgment by groups who regard themselves as marginalized. For those not content with absolute patriarchal authority, there are issues of justice in the family; these concern the equality of adult partners and the entitlements and rights of children. We can also think of environmental justice: the need to balance allocations between human beings and other living species. One writer has even referred to ontological justice. Unlike other forms of justice, ontological justice is simple to the point of being elemental; everybody enjoys the fundamental equality of dying in the end. Exactly once.

Then, of course, there's cosmic justice. That's what we would have if every man and woman were rewarded or punished—in heaven, hell, or another suitable place—exactly as appropriate to the degree of virtue or vice he or she had exhibited in life. If there is no God or other supernatural power, there is no force in the world possessing the wisdom and capacity to implement cosmic justice, so it's just an idea and will never be a reality. If there is a God, whatever be His name, that Being should be in charge of cosmic justice. It's alarming to think that human agents might presume to be agents of cosmic justice by destroying the infidel right here on earth.

At one point, President George W. Bush and his advisors had proposed to name their antiterrorist operation "Operation Infinite Justice." They dropped the label when they realized that it gravely offended Muslims, who understand "Infinite Justice" as referring to a cosmic justice better left to Allah than to U.S. military forces.

One might say, well, so what? So what if there are these things called social justice and environmental justice and justice in the family? So what if Rawls wrote a noteworthy book, and many other intellectuals talked about it, and so on? In the struggle against terrorism, isn't all this simply irrelevant? Aren't these philosophical theories just so much pedantry in the end? It's perfectly clear, one might insist, just what President George W. Bush had in mind for terrorists in general and Osama bin Laden in particular. Punishment, punishment pure and simple, punishment understood as retribution, which means bringing those who deserve the worst to a bad end. It might seem that there is a clear instinct here, a gut instinct that it's morally important to preserve. It's the instinct that Justice is done when Wrongdoers are Punished and made to Suffer, because that's what the Evildoers Deserve. And doubtless it was such an instinct that gave the rhetoric of justice its initial appeal.

But I don't think it's quite so simple. Because the social and distributive dimensions to justice and the various conceptions of penal justice turn out to be highly relevant in the end, we need to ask what this justice will be. Does justice mean the rough justice of the battlefield or justice in some court of law? If these people are going to get what they deserve, well, then, what do they deserve? How will we find out? The focus of the original appeal begins to falter when we think about these details.

In calling for justice, one might be alluding to the rough justice of the battlefield. One can understand how this idea might be defended. If you know that the people you are fighting are evil and you encounter them on the battlefield, you can bring them to justice by killing them. Isn't killing the enemy the whole point, in war? No complex issues about courts, laws, rights, and due process arise at this point—or so it might seem. These people have done the worst or supported the worst, and so they should suffer the worst. Kill them, execute them. That's it. If a Northern Alliance, American, or British soldier should encounter Osama bin Laden riding along on a horse or plotting in a cave, he should simply perform a summary execution. Just kill the man. Don't give him a trial where he would have a lawyer and an opportunity to publicize his arguments. Don't put him in prison, where he might write about his ideas or in some other way motivate supporters to stage more attacks. Get him, dead or alive—preferably dead. Execute him on the spot.

There are, of course, a few complications in the scenario. You would want to make sure the person you were executing really was Osama bin Laden, and not just somebody who looked like him. And you would want to make sure it really was bin Laden who sponsored the September 11 attacks on the United States. There are of course several videotaped statements in which bin Laden appears to take credit for those acts, including an amateurish tape featuring a casual conversation in which he seems to chortle elatedly about the destruction wrought by the hijackers. But the existence of such tapes doesn't eliminate all questions about legal and moral responsibility. Was it bin Laden on the video or someone who looked like him? Did he genuinely acknowledge his role and that of his network? Niceties? Mere niceties?

I think not. There's the crucial matter of due legal process, in which fundamental rights and liberties are properly respected in well-conducted trials. Due legal process really matters. Practices of representation by legal counsel, presentation of evidence, cross-examination, and the right to appeal are not mere formalities. Such legal practices are precious precisely because they are designed to handle questions of legal responsibility and accountability in a fair way. You can begin to appreciate the importance of due legal process by placing yourself behind the kind of veil of ignorance proposed by Rawls. Let's say you are faced with selecting the basic principles of procedural justice. From behind your veil of ignorance, you don't know whether you are a criminal, an accused criminal, an innocent person with a shaky reputation, or an innocent person with a good reputation. You would want to select principles that will protect you in any one of these circumstances—which is another way of saying that the principles of legal process should be fair to all. The point is not to be altruistic and adopt liberal-minded notions on the grounds that they will protect the rights of other people—although that would all be very nice too. Rawls urges a more basic line of thought: The "other" could be you. You could be innocent and yet charged with committing a serious offense. Just because somebody is suspected of having committed a terrible crime does not mean that he or she has no right to due legal process; everybody has that right. Perhaps people are ready to condone such things as detention without charge and the lack of public scrutiny for evidence because they assume cavalierly that "it won't happen to me." We think, "Well, I'm not male or young or brown or Middle Eastern or Muslim or Arab, so nothing like this could happen to me. I'll be all right." It's exactly the wrong approach, Rawls would say. To understand legal process, we should think of how it would look and feel to members of less-protected groups. The guiding principle, he argued, is that we should seek to maximize every person's liberty provided it does not infringe on the liberty of others.

Getting back to the dusty ruins of Afghanistan, another highly awkward question presents itself. For weeks in November and December 2001, media discussions focused on bin Laden as an individual and virtually ignored the thousands of other potential terrorists to be dealt with. There were innumerable discussions of whether U.S. forces would be able to catch bin Laden and how and where they might do it. By January 2002, the difficult issue of the many other fighters had become apparent. There were Taliban soldiers young and old—presumably with varying degrees of commitment to the cause—and there were thousands of foreign nationals, the so-called Afghan Arabs, fighting along with the Taliban. These men, often the most fierce and persistent fighters, were terrorists-in-training. They had come from many countries—

including, as it turned out, Pakistan, Saudi Arabia, Syria, Malaysia, Britain, France, Australia, and the United States itself—to train in the terrorist camps run by bin Laden and his followers. Clearly the policy of rough battlefield justice featuring summary execution could hardly be applied to all these people. To do that would be highly objectionable from a moral point of view because such rough justice would provide no opportunity to scrutinize individual responsibility. Legally it would be anathema, and politically it would provoke an outcry.

As events developed, varying approaches became apparent. There was a general sense that Afghan citizens fighting with the Taliban should be distinguished from foreigners who had come to Afghanistan specifically to join up with al-Qaeda and support terrorism. Northern Alliance forces tended to make deals with the native Afghan fighters and kill off the Arab Afghans. In February 2002, the interim government of Afghanistan released some three hundred Taliban prisoners taken in the war. Britain announced the policy of turning its captives over to the interim Afghan administration and urged the United States to return British al-Qaeda fighters to Britain so that they could be tried there. The United States was taking captured fighters to Guantanamo Bay, Cuba, for interrogation and eventual prosecution before special military tribunals authorized by the president. Canada was providing troops to assist the United States and worrying about the implications of turning over prisoners who were not considered by the United States to be prisoners of war and might not be protected by the Geneva Conventions.

The United States held that al-Qaeda and Taliban prisoners did not merit prisoner-of-war status because they were "illegal combatants." The administration issued confusing statements about the application of the Geneva Conventions. Some said that as illegal combatants the prisoners had no entitlement to protection under those conventions and wouldn't receive it; others claimed that prisoners were being treated according to those conventions, even though, strictly speaking, they were illegal combatants with no legal entitlement to such treatment. Bringing the evildoers to justice was turning out to be more complicated than anticipated.

The conundrum of fighters on the losing side recalls the situation that South Africa sought to address through its Truth and Reconciliation Commission. Widely admired outside South Africa, the TRC was nevertheless the object of considerable criticism at home. Highly prominent among criticisms was the claim that its policies were contrary to the basic principles of justice. This point was alleged most particularly because of the amnesty policy. If a person confessed his acts to the commission and fully disclosed the relevant information about them, and if those acts were thought to have been politically motivated, then that person could apply to the commission's Amnesty Committee for immunity from civil and criminal prosecution in connection with those acts. Amnesty was an individual matter; the Amnesty Committee evaluated requests one at a time. There were more than 7,000 of them, so it was a big job.

Critics of the TRC attacked its amnesty policy most of all. There were practical dimensions to this debate. Without a negotiated settlement to the conflict over apartheid, there would have been civil war; and without amnesty, there could have been no negotiated settlement between the Nationalist government and the African National Congress. Furthermore, if the thousands accused of serious human rights violations had all been given legal trials, the legal system would have been bogged down for decades, consuming resources needed for improvements in such areas as housing, health, social welfare, and employment opportunities. Thus one could defend amnesty on purely pragmatic grounds.

A few brave souls even carried the debate to the territory of justice itself, pointing out that justice has many dimensions. Two underlying assumptions had scarcely been contested in this debate—the assumption that justice was penal justice and the assumption that penal justice could be achieved through retributive punishment. Amnesty could be understood as an aspect of restorative justice. Furthermore, justice wasn't the only value relevant to South Africa's situation. There was also the matter of bringing some kind of peace to the conflict-torn country. Restorative justice could be linked to national reconciliation and the building of a sustainable peace that would make the goals of social justice more feasible.

Such considerations strike me as highly relevant to the postwar situation in Afghanistan. Barring rough justice for every Taliban soldier and Arab Afghan fighting by his side—which would require the summary execution of thousands of people—anyone thinking of penal justice as retributive must acknowledge the need for trials. That's how to determine who has done what, what his legal responsibility is, and which laws bear on the case. And surely at least some of the people involved should face trial; rough justice is not good enough. But new questions arise: Where would such proceedings take place and at what cost? Under which legal auspices? What about resources, personnel, and standards of evidence? The practical problems would be enormous—which is presumably what the interim Afghan government was thinking of when it released some three hundred Taliban prisoners in February 2002. If Afghanistan is ever to enjoy sustainable peace as a democratic country, some form of national reconciliation will be needed. The prospect of some kind of amnesty may begin to seem reasonable, although as applied to determined terrorists it is problematic. The U.S. administration has understandably tended to resist the idea. Considering the sheer number of cases and the difficulty of thoroughly investigating them, the instinctive appeal of retributive justice begins to diminish. The much-discussed issue of bin Laden as an individual may begin to appear simple by comparison.

Still, let's return to that case. An Internet poll was taken on November 21, 2001, on the question of what should happen to

Osama bin Laden if he is captured. Of some 200,000 responses, 70 percent supported summary execution as opposed to legal trial. I find this result alarming in its disregard for due legal process. Perhaps many of those polled believed that bin Laden was such a terrible character and had committed such terrible crimes that he had thrown away all his rights, including the right he might have to a fair trial. But that would be a misunderstanding. Nobody throws away his right to due legal process. That's the whole point; we don't make exceptions for cases we think are special. It's a fundamental element of the rule of law.

Other people calling for bin Laden and other al-Qaeda leaders to be "brought to justice" were clearly thinking about legal justice and some kind of trial. There was considerable discussion about what sort of court would be suitable and whether the military tribunals authorized by President George W. Bush would provide sufficient protections for the rights of the accused. In theory, bin Laden, like Serbia's Milosevic, could be brought to an international court. But such a court would have to be established particularly for the purpose. The two existing war crimes tribunals—one in The Hague, the other in Arusha, Kenya—have specific jurisdictions for crimes committed in the former Yugoslavia and Rwanda. An international criminal court is in the making but it is not yet operative; one reason for this is that the United States has opposed the initiative because it does not want an internationally authorized body to have jurisdiction over the actions of its military personnel. Another possibility would be to try bin Laden in a civilian court in the United States. The attacks were committed on U.S. soil, and other terrorists have been successfully prosecuted and tried in the United States. In a nonmilitary U.S. court, bin Laden would enjoy the protections of due legal process. In a secret tribunal, informed public scrutiny of the evidence and arguments would be impossible, potentially valuable information about terrorist networks would be removed from public scrutiny, and due legal process would not be guaranteed.

Highly relevant at this point is the old adage that justice should not only be done but also be seen to be done. Obviously, if a trial is held in secret, no one can see how justice is being done in that trial. In this context, many observers at home and abroad simply wouldn't believe the trial to be just. If it were to occur, this would be a trial by the world's remaining superpower of the world's most powerful radical Islamist leader for allegedly masterminding heavily damaging attacks.

But ignore these awkward problems for a moment. Let's return to the theme of bringing people to justice and make lots of assumptions. Assume that bin Laden will be captured. Assume that justice is penal justice, and penal justice is retribution, and retribution is giving somebody what he deserves, and bin Laden is somebody who deserves the worst, a very harsh punishment indeed, and that punishment can be fairly imposed and administered by a secret U.S. military tribunal. Then let's think about it. If this man really did plot and sponsor the murder of some 3,100 people, bringing serious harm to thousands more, what *does* he deserve? Many people argue on retributive grounds for capital punishment in the case of murder. They say that because a murderer has violated someone else's right to life, he should lose his own life. A life for a life. But how could such proportionality be achieved if someone was involved in mass murderer?

Die-hard advocates of retribution might argue at this point that bin Laden and others like him should, well, die hard. Maybe summary execution is wrong for a different reason: It would be too generous to such persons. Should they be made to suffer years of agonizing torture before their deaths? Or sentenced to 3,100 life-terms of punitively hard labor? Ideas of retribution run into problems here: A person may have killed many others but he cannot himself die many times as a punishment for his crimes. Every human being has exactly one life to lose and can lose it exactly once. Retributive justice bumps into ontological justice at this point, and the retributive idea of a punishment that fits the crime breaks down. Multiple sentences can be issued, but they don't alter the fundamental fact. To make a person suffer "equally" would commit authorities to imposing barbarities upon him; when the deaths and suffering of thousands are involved, there just doesn't seem to be enough suffering that could be imposed on one human being. Furthermore, there are powerful reasons against authorizing and maintaining institutions empowered to try and convict someone secretly and then impose extraordinarily severe penalties— especially when one's goal in doing so is to defend a democratic society that exemplifies the values of Western civilization and operates under the rule of law.

Authorities can't give serial murders what they deserve because their crimes are so terrible that we can't really say what they deserve. And even if we could, we wouldn't know how to impose the penalty in a nonbarbaric fashion. Just something awful—but how would anyone bring it about? The mind boggles.

Yes, justice should be done. These people should be brought to justice. But the rhetoric of justice has not furthered our understanding of key questions about courts, rules, and fair procedures. In its tendency to conflate justice, battlefield justice, and badly administered retributive punishment, such talk is an obstacle to careful thinking about the many dimensions of justice.

Notes

John Rawls, in *A Theory of Justice* (Cambridge, Mass.: Harvard University Press, 1971), submits a theory intended to apply to one society only. Whether Rawls should, from consistency, support a conception of global distributive justice extending beyond the bounds of any given society has been much debated. Some have argued for the implication, but Rawls denies it. A relevant description of the issue may be found in Chris Brown, "John Rawls, the Law of People, and International Political Theory," *Ethics and International Affairs* 14 (2000): 125–132. For my understanding of the South African Truth and Reconciliation Commission, I owe much to my extensive discussions and collaboration with

W. J. Verwoerd, who served for several years on its research staff. Reflections on the work of the TRC may be found in Charles Villa-Vicencio and Wilhelm Verwoerd, eds., *Looking Back, Reaching Forward: Reflections on the Truth and Reconciliation Commission of South Africa* (Cape Town: University of Cape Town Press, 2000); and in Desmond Tutu, *No Future Without Forgiveness* (New York: Doubleday, 1999). A detailed and helpful discussion of the issues in domestic and international law posed by the Guantanamo Bay situation and the military tribunals is that of Aryeh Neier, "The Military Tribunals on Trial," *New York Review of Books,* February 14, 2002, 11–14.

As noted earlier, bin Laden had not been captured as of January 2004. Some of the same issues arise regarding Saddam Hussein. There seemed to be agreement that a trial would be needed, and what would be most appropriate would be a trial by Iraqis, who had been most victimized by his regime. However, no details had been arranged. The United States released some prisoners from Guantanamo, though over six hundred were still being held, according to a British Broadcasting Corporation report on January 20, 2004. The International Criminal Court was established in The Hague and had begun to function, but it was not supported by the United States and thus seemed not to be a candidate for trying Saddam Hussein.

8

VIOLENCE

Getting a consistent moral stance on violence is a tricky matter, and the inconsistencies of our culture don't help. We tend to criticize violence and admire it at the same time. People decry the violence of terrorists and violent criminals; yet most support the use of military force in campaigns abroad, and many purchase guns to defend themselves. School bullies and high school shootings are deemed shocking, but video games and movies with themes of violence are popular. Violent conflict makes a good story, it seems, and gives an especially dramatic ending. Things could be pretty dull without it.

Violence is the use of physical force to damage or destroy life or property; and for all our cultural vacillations, there does seem to be some rough consensus that violence is wrong. Or, other things being equal, violence is wrong. Or, it is generally wrong, though sometimes it's right. Or acceptable. Or at least excusable.

Violence mostly occurs in contexts of conflict. It's one kind of response to conflict, that of using physical force against others in an attempt to dominate other people and end the conflict in our own way. We experience conflicts because we have goals that are incompatible, or seem to be incompatible; these differing goals arise from differing beliefs, values, interests, or needs. Conflict between human beings is an inevitable feature of human life and engaging in conflicts may bring valuable changes. But violence in response to conflict is not inevitable; there are lots of other possible responses. If you have a conflict, well, you can ignore it, manage your life so that it disappears, or try to resolve the issue verbally. You can seek a compromise, bring in a friend to help you, consult a professional mediator, have a lawyer negotiate with the other party, and, as a last resort, go to court. If a husband and wife consult a marriage counselor to work out their difficulties or resort to lawyers to arrange a divorce, that's socially acceptable. If he beats her to try to get his way, that's not. On the popular *Frasier* television comedy show, a character declared, "I'm a lawyer; when I get hurt, I sue." This was extreme but still within the bounds of decent behavior: he wasn't going to go out and kill somebody. Something comparable is true even for relations between nation-states. Negotiations, treaties, and contracts are far less controversial than war. For all our fascination with cultural products exalting violence, we generally assume that violent means to our ends can be justified only as a last resort—if at all.

And it's easy to see why. Violence is damaging by definition. It destroys property, damages the environment and sentient creatures, and endangers, injures, and kills human beings. And it's risky; those who use it may die by it. Notoriously, violence tends to inspire further violence. Resorting to violence when conflict arises results in destruction, pain, and death; eventually it culminates in victory by the physically strongest party. Such victory has nothing to do with moral or legal entitlements. Physical strength may allow one party to prevail in a conflict that has become violent, but it has nothing to do with the rightness or legality of its cause. It's an understatement to say that violence is a poor technique for conflict resolution. The truth is, it's not a technique for conflict resolution at all. Violence doesn't resolve conflicts in the long term because it doesn't address the underlying differences between the people involved. What might superficially appear to be the military resolution of some problem has little sustainability if it's divorced from moral or legal principles. Even in cases where a conflict seems to have ended because one party is destroyed, the "solution" is likely to be illusory because the defeated party will have descendants and affiliates who spring forward to take up the cause. A world in which conflicts are resolved by violence will not be a world of reason or justice. Were violence between citizens not illegal—and relatively rare—we could hardly live together at all.

So violence is not to be taken lightly, and its use requires a compelling moral justification. Such justifications typically involve arguments to the effect that our ends are worthy and violence is necessary as the only possible means to achieve them. The basic line of argument tends to be something like this: we have to achieve this thing, and we can't do it in any other way. Self-defense is probably the clearest example. Common morality has it that if we are attacked, we are morally justified in killing the attacker in self-defense if that is the only way to prevent the attacker from killing us. Or, if one's child is being attacked, a violent response is justified then, too—provided there is no other way to save the child. If our property is attacked, is violence justified? That's more debatable.

The political level is highly complex. If a country is attacked, are its citizens morally justified in killing its attackers in self-defense? All but total pacifists would answer this question with a firm yes. But if those attackers are already dead, is that country justified in killing people affiliated with the first attackers, provided those affiliated people indicated that they were intending and planning further attacks? Or other people in a repressive state harboring these affiliated people? Could a kind of preemptive self-defense be justified if political leaders believed that bombing the harboring state was necessary to prevent further attacks on their country? Many would say yes, obviously. Of course. It's still self-defense because they would be preventing an attack on themselves. Others would be more cautious and ask about the evidence and how the affiliated people, the sheltering state and civilians within it, were linked with the original attackers.

To say that questions about the legitimacy of political attacks are difficult is a considerable understatement; indeed, theologians, philosophers, and strategists have long sought credible theories in response. In the Western tradition, versions of Just War Theory provide a respected tradition of answers. Stemming from the work of St. Augustine, Just War Theory was subsequently developed by Thomas Aquinas and many other thinkers and is still widely discussed today. Just War Theory comes in two parts. The first, concerning the justifiability of going to war in the first place, is called *jus ad bellum*. The second, concerning the justice of the means used to wage war, is called *jus in bello*. *Jus ad bellum* requires that a just war be waged for a just cause; that it be undertaken as a last resort; that it have a reasonable chance of success; that it be declared by a proper authority; and that it be proportionate to the ends sought. (That is, what is sacrificed in the war must not be disproportionate to what one is trying to gain.) *Jus in bello* concerns campaigns and strategies within the war; here, too, it is required that there be a proportionality of costs and gains. The most important aspect of *jus in bello* is the distinction between combatants and civilians, the principle being that because it is the combatants who constitute a threat to one's security, it is morally permissible to intentionally kill combatants—but not noncombatants. Deaths of noncombatants, or civilians, are morally undesirable; they should never be deliberately sought and are tolerable only when they are unavoidable side effects of legitimate military tactics. (This restriction is the source of the notion of collateral damage.) In a just war, civilian deaths must be kept to a minimum.

The Just War Theory is still taught in contemporary military academies in the United States and elsewhere, and political and military leaders appeal to it with greater and lesser degrees of sincerity. Obviously, the theory originated in a world very different from our own. Many questions arise when we try to apply this venerable theory to today's world. What is a just cause? Can both sides in a war have a just cause? What is a legitimate authority for declaring war, either in an oppressive state or in a state whose very existence is the subject of the war? The theory was devised for wars between states, but many wars—virtually all of them since 1989—have been within states. How well does the theory apply to situations of revolutionary violence, or contexts in which an ethnic or religious group seeks to separate from an existing state and found a state of its own? What are the alternatives to war? How many of them have to be explored, and with what degree of seriousness, before war can be justified as a "last resort"? What would constitute "success" in a war? Would having a reasonable chance of success just mean having a reasonable chance of winning a military victory? Or would it require having a reasonable chance of creating a sustainable peace in the aftermath of the war?

Weapons such as bombs and antipersonnel land mines don't do a very good job of distinguishing between combatants and civilians. And reminding the public that modern weapons are "smart" will hardly solve the problem. An even more embarrassing matter for Just War Theory is the presumed correlation between noncombatant status and the kind of innocence that makes a person an unfit target for military attack. This correlation is questionable. Combatants can include young soldiers—and even, in some appalling cases, children who have been cruelly recruited or abducted and share no responsibility for the political decisions underlying the war. At the same time, not all noncombatants are innocent and uninvolved. Noncombatants may include civilians who make munitions or contribute to war propaganda. They may be respectable older citizens who wear good suits and sit in tidy offices where they plan the war or profit from weapons sales while witnessing with calm and impunity the deaths of the young. It's stretching things to regard such people as innocent if you assume that the war they are contributing to as noncombatants is not being waged for a good cause.

I gather that the conception of *jihad* within Islam has at least one striking similarity to Just War Theory. It's open to many interpretations. *Jihad*, it seems, can be interpreted as a struggle against temptations within oneself or as a war against an external enemy. And the Islamic tradition incorporates fine distinctions between suicide and martyrdom that are likely to strike a Western observer as contrived and bizarre. Suicide is terribly wrong and something to be ashamed of; martyrdom, on the other hand, is not suicide at all, and it is heroically, eternally admirable. One man's suicide bomber is another man's martyr. Killing innocent people is wrong, but resisting imperialist oppression is admirable. (And if the latter requires the former, what then?) There are no Palestinian suicide bombers on this analysis; these people are resistance fighters who heroically seek the liberation of their people from Israeli oppression. They may even be religious martyrs defending a holy religion that has been terribly persecuted and subject to ongoing attacks. The distinctions seem arbitrary; they're every bit as contestable as some of our own.

When can political agents justifiably resort to violence and war? How can we draw a reasonable line between justifiable and unjustifiable recourse to violence? In my pessimistic moments, I sometimes think it's not possible to work out a Just War Theory for modern times. It seems sometimes that there are only two consistent responses to the problem of political violence: total pacifism and total realpolitik. To the question, "When is political violence justified?" total pacifism answers, "Never." Never ever. It simply isn't justified, and that's the end of the story. The conflicts that are inevitable in human life won't be resolved by violence, so we have to develop means of nonviolent conflict resolution.

Total realpolitik answers, "Always." Whenever we like. If violence is the means we need, or think we need, to defend our interests, we can go ahead and use it and destroy whatever and whoever gets in our way. Violence in politics is just one means among others—as Karl von Clausewitz said in his remark that war is politics by other means. This is how the world works: by force, by persuasion, by law, or by justice. If you've got it, use it; go forth and take what you want.

We can think of a spectrum of views about the justifiability of political violence and put total pacifism at one end and total realpolitik at the other. "The truth must lie somewhere in the middle," most people would say, being neither Quakers nor Fascists. Just War Theory seems to help us chart out that comfortable middle territory, which is part of its appeal. But explaining why and when and where it is all right to kill other people in contexts of political conflict is a profoundly difficult matter. Many temptations arise along the way. An especially ubiquitous one is that of bias in favor of our own side. We have an inclination to think with an Our Side Bias that makes us brand all violence used against us as appalling and evil; but at the same time we justify our own violence as necessary and good. If we are doing it, it must be justifiable, because it's "us." If we are suffering from it, it must be deplorable, because it's "them"—and they are our enemies. Our Side Bias allows us to find reasons for our own violence while we decry violence employed against us. It makes for an arrogant and self-indulgent account and one that won't meet standards of moral consistency.

If we're not content with total pacifism or total realpolitik and we want to transcend Our Side Bias, we are left with the messy challenge of trying to find a version of Just War Theory that applies to today's world. In a world of rebel groups, states of questionable legitimacy, arms trading, child soldiers, weapons of mass destruction, cluster bombs, and land mines, it's hard to apply Just War

Theory in a plausible way. Charting that middle territory on the spectrum is no easy matter.

But a solution suggests itself. Let's make a word do the work. "Terrorism." Stop all this talk about the justifiability of violence as a last resort. Stop worrying about whether modern wars in general—or one contemporary war in particular—are right or wrong. Or how many alternatives to war there are, or whether there are states so awful that nobody can exercise legitimate authority. Forget the awful details: the child soldiers forced to amputate limbs from villagers in Sierra Leone, the damaging land mines, the toxic aftereffects of depleted uranium, the nuclear almost-threats. The aftereffects of the cold war, the trading in arms large and small. We may not agree about violence and war, but the solution is at hand because we agree about something else. Terrorism. We know what terrorism is, after all; terrorism is airplane hijackings, attacks on buildings, bombs in cars and markets. Some of us were direct victims of it and all of us were afraid. Terrorism is wrong, clearly, absolutely, fundamentally wrong, and universally acknowledged to be so. So if we wage war against terrorism and fight evil, we'll be sure to be right—and the problem of political violence will be solved. There's a rhetoric and a theory about just wars, but terrorism is presumed to be wrong by definition. We don't hear people talking about just terrorism; there's no venerable tradition of just terrorism.

What is terrorism? There's some agreement. First, terrorist techniques employ physical violence; the goal is to damage or destroy civilians and the structures of civilian society, and sometimes military facilities within it. Second, the intent of this violent destruction is to spread terror in the society in question; that is to say, frighten and intimidate ordinary people as they go about their ordinary lives. Third, all this is done for some political goal or cause. The IRA (Irish Republican Army) used terrorist methods and was a terrorist group. So was the Palestine Liberation Organization. So were the

Israelis under Menachem Begin when, in 1946, they bombed the King David Hotel, killing some eighty-six people. So, too, are the Basques in Spain, the Tamil Tigers in Sri Lanka, the Islamic militants in Kashmir, the Kurds in Turkey, the Kurds in Iraq, and many other groups.

But the descriptive core of meaning doesn't suffice to explain how people actually use the word "terrorism" to draw moral distinctions about political violence. That's because it leaves open questions about who is using this violence and for what purpose. Given the assumption that terrorism is wrong, most people refuse to call political violence "terrorism" when they approve of it. So the agreement we thought we had about terrorism turns out to be more superficial than we would like. The word doesn't make controversies about justifying violence go away. To be sure, just about everybody claims to be against terrorism—but people disagree about whether some particular political violence amounts to terrorism. The term *terrorism* has a core of descriptive content; but, in addition, it is used to express value judgments—and because people disagree about those value judgments, they apply the term differently. Thus the familiar saying that one man's terrorist is another man's freedom fighter.

In early November 2001, Irish Republican Army leader Gerry Adams was in North America to raise funds for his cause. Questioned in a radio interview about the terrorist past of the IRA, Adams denied that it had one. Listeners must have been surprised to learn that this group, which had over several decades bombed restaurants and cars, killing hundreds of people in Northern Ireland and the mainland United Kingdom, had never been a terrorist organization. Their surprise could only have increased when Adams mentioned that although he had never been a terrorist or a member of a terrorist group, he could mention one other famous person who had. That was South Africa's revered former president, Nelson Mandela. Now this was a rather clever rhetorical cover-up

on Adams' part: The audience was supposed to infer a kind of
virtue by association between Gerry Adams and a beloved world
figure. (We can hope that listeners were too clever to swallow the
fallacy.)

Was Nelson Mandela once a terrorist? In the early 1960s, before
his long prison term, Mandela supported property violence against
the structures of the apartheid state that was his home country.
Those would have been terrorist methods. Of course Mandela was
in jail when the African National Congress was fighting against the
apartheid state, so he never personally committed acts of violence
against his fellow South Africans, white or black. At the hearings of
the Truth and Reconciliation Commission, the African National
Congress never admitted that it had engaged in terrorism, but it
acknowledged that it had committed politically motivated acts of
violence against the apartheid state. In fact, the ANC claimed it
fought a just war.

Several weeks later, Mandela visited North America. He gave a
speech in which he argued that recourse to violence against an
extremely oppressive state was sometimes necessary as a last resort.
Listeners were shocked and appalled. Was this venerated moral
leader identifying himself with terrorists? The provocative speech
was a reminder that the moral problems about political violence
aren't going to be resolved by using the word "terrorism."

Who is a terrorist? Who was once a terrorist? What is the moral
difference between a terrorist who thinks he has adopted political
violence as a justified last resort and a person who is engaged in
waging a just war? Is the first one always unjustified and wrong,
and the second one always justified and right? Mandela suggested
a solution: Resolve the contest in favor of the winners. If your
resistance group uses violent means successfully to unseat an
oppressive government and replaces that government, gaining
world recognition as the new government, well then, people will
invite you to state dinners and the like. They won't say you are a

terrorist and they will be polite enough never to remind you that you used to be one, and at that point, you won't be a terrorist any more. That happened to Menachem Begin, Yasser Arafat, and (on his telling of the story) Mandela himself. If you don't win your struggle and if you've used violence against civilians as a means in your political campaign, you are not going to become a respected member of a recognized government. You remain a terrorist.

Preferences in using the word "terrorist" tell us a lot. Egyptian clerics earnestly explain how Palestinians bombing shops and streets in Israel are not terrorists. Indeed, those we call suicide bombers do not commit suicide when they kill themselves. Because they die resisting the wrongful oppression of Muslim people by Jews, they die in martyrdom, which is something else entirely. The clerics interviewed by an American journalist shortly after the September 11 attacks did not seek to justify them—unlike some radical Islamist supporters, who did. For these people, the attacks didn't amount to terrorism; they were the integral stages of a holy war.

Many persons of Irish descent in North America supported the IRA. They were supporting a terrorist group when they did so, in the belief that somehow Irish Catholics had to get out from under the heels of Protestants. Even allowing for several degrees of self-deception, many of these donors must have known that the IRA used violent methods. Did its recourse to political violence amount to terrorism? Of course. Was it morally justified? I doubt it—but I won't pontificate on the matter here.

The United Nations has been trying to define terrorism for some thirty years, and has given up in its quest for a definition that everybody can agree upon. A major problem is that Western governments wanted to make sure that state agents could never be considered terrorist, while Islamic countries wanted to make sure that national liberation movements in the Middle East and Kashmir could never be considered terrorist.

How could we solve the problem of defining "terrorism"? We could make an open appeal to Our Side Bias and say that political violence amounts to terrorism provided we disagree with it. That's a self-indulgent double standard. We could follow Mandela's suggestion and allow success to make the difference. That's too after-the-fact to be useful and too relativistic to be morally credible. It's not clear, in fact, that Mandela meant the suggestion seriously; I suspect he was being sarcastic. Another possibility is to permit the distinction between state and nonstate agents to make the difference on the grounds that only *states* are authorized to employ violent means in political conflicts. Fundamentally, this is the stance of U.S. State Department, which by definition regards terrorism as an illegitimate use of violence by nonstate agents, who employ it for political purposes.

In 1998, the U.S. State Department said, "The term 'terrorism' means premeditated politically motivated violence perpetrated against noncombatant targets by sub-national groups or clandestine agents, usually intended to influence an audience." Terrorism is perpetrated by nonstate agents. On this theory, so-called terrorist states do not commit terrorist acts directly; rather, they fund or assist terrorists by helping with such matters as passports and accommodations and supplying weapons. On these assumptions, if nonstate groups use political violence to intimidate others and pursue their goals, they are terrorists and what they do is absolutely unjustified. If states do use political violence in pursuit of their goals, they are not terrorists. Even if innocent civilians are injured and killed along the way, what these states do may be justified provided their actions satisfy the requirements of a just war. According to this understanding, Palestinian suicide bombers are terrorists, but Israeli troops who enter Palestinian villages to destroy houses and kill suspected terrorists are not terrorists. By definition, they couldn't be terrorists because they are identified agents of a legitimate state.

Tony Blair must have had something like this in mind when he toured the Middle East in November 2001. Seeking to consolidate the coalition in the war against terrorism, Blair visited President Assad of Syria. He was shocked to discover that the consensus about terrorism was not as solid as he had thought. Amazingly, Assad appeared to believe that Palestinians who killed themselves while bombing Israeli targets were resistance fighters courageously seeking the liberation of their people and weren't terrorists at all. This wasn't quite the kind of solid consensus that Blair and his colleague George W. Bush had been banking on. But the British prime minister didn't blink and he didn't blush. He went right on to lecture the Syrians about the evils of all terrorism, at the same time defending the bombing of Afghanistan by the United Kingdom and the United States.

So what about this solution, based on the assumptions that only nonstate agents can be terrorists and that terrorism is always wrong whereas state agents can wage wars that are sometimes just wars and morally right? I don't find it credible. Like Our Side Bias, this account is based on a double standard. And the double standard is objectionable because it utterly neglects to consider the manifest inadequacy and illegitimacy of some states. With its gross denial of civil rights to more than 80 percent of its people, apartheid South Africa was a case in point. Still more fundamentally, this state-biased definition is objectionable because it's morally arbitrary. Why should the nature of the *agent*—for example, a state represented by individuals wearing uniforms—make a morally questionable *means* good? The real issue is the killing of innocent people in the pursuit of one's political goals.

The moral problem with terrorism is that terrorists frighten and kill civilian people and societies who are caught in the middle of serious political conflicts when the terrorists resort to violence for political ends. The moral problem with war (just or otherwise) is that soldiers frighten and kill innocent people and societies who get caught in the middle—you get the picture. The awkward and devastating truth about political violence is that innocent people do get killed when it's going on, and many of those who aren't killed are vulnerable and frightened and harmed in the general mayhem. And the moral dilemmas of political violence arise if we want to argue that sometimes—but only sometimes—this killing of the innocent is justified. Appeals to the evil of terrorism won't make this thorny problem go away.

Notes

The discussions of suicide and martyrdom in Islam were reported by Joseph Lelyveld in "What Makes a Suicide Bomber? His Psyche Is the Least of It," *New York Times Magazine*, October 28, 2001. A thorough discussion of Just War Theory is given by Jeff McMahon and Robert McKim in "The Just War and the Gulf War," *Canadian Journal of Philosophy* 23:4 (1993): 501–541. The idea of a spectrum of views on the ethics of war is taken from Duane L. Cady, *From Warism to Pacifism: A Moral Continuum* (Philadelphia: Temple University Press, 1989). Gerry Adams was quoted widely when he visited North America in mid-November, 2001; I heard him interview on the "As It Happens" radio program on the CBC. Nelson Mandela's comments were made in a speech he gave to the Canadian House of Commons on the occasion he was made an honorary citizen (November 25, 2001). The U.S. State Department definition of "terrorism" (1998) was cited in Neve Gordon and George A. Lopez, "Terrorism in the Arab-Israeli Conflict," chap. 7 in Andrew Valls, ed., *Ethics in International Affairs: Theories and Cases* (Lanham, Md.: Rowman and Littlefield, 2000). They object to the double standard in the 1998 State Department definition.

It is, of course, disputable whether military killings of noncombatants should be seen as morally similar to terrorist killings of noncombatants. This is crucial topic in the understanding of political violence. Defenders of Just War Theory would firmly deny the analogy I make in this essay on the grounds that, in fighting a just war, military planners and soldiers do whatever they can to avoid killing noncombatants and to minimize such killings if they are unavoidable. At a conference on Understanding Terrorism held at Loyola Marymount University, September 11–13, 2003, several philosophers employed by the United States military argued the position that while terrorists kill noncombatants intentionally and maximally, the military kills them only after great effort not to do so, and minimally. They denied any moral equivalence between terrorists and the military of a state engaged in a just war, with regard to the killing of noncombatants. So too did Daniel Statman, an Israeli philosopher at the same event, who defended his country's practice of the targeted killing of Palestinian militants. At the same time, philosophers have begun to discuss the question whether, if there are *just wars*, there could be any such thing as *just terrorism*.

9

RESPONSIBILITY

"The root causes of terrorism." From an academic point of view, it's probably an endless topic. From a political point of view, it's far more sensitive than you'd think. In the aftermath of the September 11 attacks, calling for understanding of the root causes of terrorism has been controversial, to put it mildly. For the most part, only a few dove-ish souls towards the left of the political spectrum have issued this call. Many others have found it terribly offensive. Why?

The idea seems to be something like this. Root causes would be conditions such as poverty, lack of opportunity, absence of institutions permitting democratic political participation, simplistic and intolerant ideologies, resentment and envy, real or perceived inadequacies in U.S. foreign policy, and the like. To say there are root causes of terrorism is to point to factors apart from individual terrorist agents and Osama bin Laden and other higher-ups in the al-Qaeda network. Political and military leaders have said nothing about the need to address root causes. A practical reason for the omission is that such considerations imply the need for a long time frame—a conception that is rarely popular in a crisis situation. But I don't think this problem is the main reason for the unpopularity of the "root causes" idea. Rather, it's the fact that the idea of root causes seems to diminish the blameworthiness of the terrorists as individuals while implying blameworthiness on the part of the

United States and other Western nations. The notion that there are root causes of terrorism suggests an excuse for the perpetrators, the implication being that they are victims of poverty, alienation, and the like—while at the same time implying that the real victims share responsibility and have some work to do. Such implications seem dreadfully inappropriate to most of those shocked and fearful in the aftermath of the attacks and in no mood to reflect seriously on deep problems.

And yet, to ignore root causes is dangerous. The reason is simple. If there are root causes of terrorism, there are conditions in which terrorist methods will strike many people as a suitable means of addressing their needs and problems. Given such conditions, even the killing of every al-Qaeda terrorist on earth wouldn't keep Western societies safe. If the underlying causal conditions are not changed, more terrorists will be trained and motivated. They will emerge from circles of dissidents opposing undemocratic regimes in Arab countries, from middle-class suburbs in Egypt and Lebanon, from apartments in France and England, from townhouses in Germany, from refugee camps in the West Bank, from *madrassas* in Pakistan—and from communities of alienated persons in the United States. You can set out with the idea that you are going to eradicate terrorism, but if there are powerful factors making terrorist methods seem necessary and reasonable to many people and you do nothing about them—refusing even to consider what they might be—you are undermining your own quest. Archbishop Desmond Tutu expressed this concern; questioning the belief that violence could provide long-term security, he said, "Retaliation against a suicide bomber only gives rise to more suicide bombers."

It's useful here to think about the word "root" in the expression "root causes." It's a suggestive metaphor. Terrorist ideologies and actions arise from conditions of resentment and intolerance that make violence seem necessary and right. Poverty, lack of demo-

cratic political power, resentment, hatred, and a casual acceptance
of violence are among the conditions that breed terrorism. If those
factors are not addressed, the roots of terrorism will remain. One
might think of killing individual terrorists as pulling plants out of
the soil, yanking them away from their roots. Doing this won't
eliminate terrorism because the roots are left behind to support
new growth. The advice to "get to the root of the problem" applies
suggestively to this picture. If we try to eradicate terrorism but
refuse to consider its roots because we don't want to contemplate
the possibility that we might share responsibility, we are doomed
to frustration in our quest. Any success we experience will be tem-
porary at best because for every terrorist we eliminate, more will
grow up to take his or her place. That's what Tutu was worried
about.

Radical Islamists are not shy about explaining their hatred of
Jews, Americans, and other Western people. Consider, for instance,
the statement made on the founding of the World Islamic Front for
Jihad Against the Jews and Crusaders that called on every Muslim to
kill Americans and steal their money "anywhere, any time, and
whenever possible." The presence of "Christian legions" in the
Arabian peninsula, the "land of the two holy places," is said to be a
humiliating disaster for Muslims. And the sanctions policy against
Iraq is considered an example of "horrifying massacres." In its support for Israel, the United States is said to have sponsored the occupation of the Muslim Holy Land and the killing of Muslim peoples
there. Other statements echo these themes: U.S. troops and Western
involvement in Saudi Arabia, policy toward Iraq, and support for
Israel in its conflict with the Palestinians. For Muslims, Saudi Arabia
is a country of holy places and a sanctified territory that should not
be patrolled by non-Muslims. In the background of all this are the
support by the United States for undemocratic governments in
Muslim countries and the grinding and infuriating poverty of hundreds of millions of Muslims who, as they struggle for subsistence,

see the affluence of the United States flagrantly displayed on television. The economic inequity is so profound that it amounts to humiliation and desperation on the part of many poor people who have little opportunity for work and a decent life. Resentment of Western power and arrogance is a powerful element in this picture. Those who want to eliminate terrorist threats should look again at the policies and attitudes that are providing the roots and replenishing the soil. To the extent that foreign and economic policies inspire such hatred, one might consider whether they should be revised. Does the United States really need Saudi oil so much that it needs to deploy troops in that country? Could more modern educational institutions be encouraged by educated Muslims working through such institutions as the Aga Khan Foundation?

Among many Muslims, there is a widespread sense of alienation from Western cultures with their secularism, pluralism, and liberated women. Many Muslims feel threatened by the power of Western peoples and cultures in a globalizing economy. A highly relevant factor is the power of the *mullahs* who teach in schools that serve to indoctrinate an intolerance characteristic of fundamentalist doctrines; such doctrines are founded on the conviction that one is absolutely right and, therefore, anyone who disagrees is absolutely wrong. In such a framework of belief, there is no room for doubt about the words and intentions of Allah about martyrdom or paradise or the evil "infidels" who constitute a powerful threat to which the only response is destruction. Terrorism, as urged by al-Qaeda and other *jihadic* groups, seems the only answer.

To say that we should reflect on the root causes of terrorism is not to say that we should change whatever it is that terrorists object to. For citizens in liberal societies, human rights and practices of tolerance, free inquiry, and the liberation of women should not be compromised just because somebody else despises them. Nor is it to say that we should accept the view that the West, and the United States in particular, ought to accept blame for everything that is wrong in undemocratic Muslim countries. Regimes in those countries, and those who support them, must share that responsibility; so must the educational authorities who have chosen to omit mathematics, sciences, history, and foreign languages from their curricula and encourage young men to commit acts of violence against the "infidels" as a quick route to paradise.

Still, there are puzzles in all this. It seems that we have reasons to reject and reasons to accept calls to study the root causes of terrorism. The dilemma recalls the arguments of Kant's "Transcendental Dialectic." In Kant's philosophy, the "Dialectic" was an exploration of forms of human reasoning that apparently enable us to prove each of two contradictory claims. Kant called the resulting paradoxes antinomies. In fact, one of his antinomies involved causation and moral responsibility. It seems we can prove first that everything that happens in this world is fully caused by previous events; and second, that every human action is produced by the free choice of some moral agent. In other words, there seem to be proofs both for full causation and for its opposite—a form of human freedom that lies outside the realm of causation. Kant thought of it this way: If Reason could really demonstrate both a thesis and an antithesis (in direct contradiction to each other), wouldn't that prove that something was desperately wrong with Reason itself? If we can't rely on Reason when we try to think things through, what can we rely on? For anyone who wants to continue to rely on Reason as a guide to knowledge and understanding, such contradictions have to be resolved somehow. That's why Kant took the antinomies so seriously.

In reflecting on the struggle against terrorism, we seem to produce a kind of Antinomy of Terrorism. First, it seems that we can prove a thesis, the statement that we *should not* explore root causes, because when we do so, we inappropriately exonerate the perpetrators and blame the victim. But then it seems we can prove an antithesis, the statement that we *should* seek out these root causes, because otherwise these factors will persist to support the growth of more terrorism and doom our quest to eradicate terrorism. It appears to be a contradiction. And the problem here is political as well as intellectual.

Here's my modest proposal for the Antinomy of Terrorism. The root causes of terrorism should be understood as standing conditions that are *necessary* for terrorism to emerge in its present form, but not *sufficient* to explain the motivations and actions of individual agents. Things such as foreign policies, repressive governments, deficiencies in educational institutions, resentments and humiliation, and religiously grounded hatred really are underlying causes of anti-American and anti-Western terrorism. These factors provide the contexts in which Islamist terrorists and terrorism grow. They have a genuine causal role, they are not irrelevant, and they provide part of the explanation of the events of September 11 and other anti-American and anti-Western attacks. Terrorism is not merely a form of evil that surfaces as a result of the insane or monstrous nature of some few aberrant individuals. But the causal factors that are necessary in generating contemporary forms of anti-Western terrorism are not sufficient to explain it. They cannot completely explain particular events because they make no reference to the feelings, beliefs, goals, and decisions of the individual agents who act. They tell us nothing about why a particular agent makes the choices he does and acts as he does. As individuals, we always act in some context—but nevertheless we bear individual responsibility for our choices and actions. I suggest, then, that the solution to the Antinomy of Terrorism lies in the compatibility of root causes, as background causes, with individual responsibility. They are necessary causes, and to fully explain what happens, we need to add the factors of individual choice.

The musical *West Side Story* contains a song, "Gee Officer Krupke," which cleverly illustrates the subtle interaction of causation and choice. Gang members in the drama are stopped by a

police officer and appeal to the "root causes" of juvenile delinquency in an effort to justify or excuse themselves. They are by no
means stupid, and they know how to exploit social theories about
causes in making their argument. Their "mothers all are junkies,"
their "fathers all are drunks"; that's why they're punks—and mis-
understood, but "deep down inside us there is good." There are
issues of environment: "My sister has a moustache, my brother
wears a dress . . . no wonder I'm a mess." They were deprived of a
normal home. "Hey, I'm depraved on account of I'm deprived."
And furthermore, they're sociologically sick; they have a social disease and should be taken to a social worker. "It's not I'm anti-social,
I'm only anti-work." And so it goes.

I used to think this song was a clear appeal to the root causes of
juvenile delinquency and expressed a kind of social determinism.
But recently I paid closer attention to the lyrics and concluded that
my first impression was superficial. The song is a pointed satire of
theories that excuse gang behavior; it shows how these characters
exploit the conceptions of "root causes" and the professionals who
are trying to "help." It's an ingenious satire of excuses based on simplistic thinking about responsibility and background causes. At the
end of their encounter with Officer Krupke, the gang members are
left asking what to do next. They have exploited theories in an
attempt to manipulate Office Krupke, but the point remains that it
is they who will have to decide what to do with their lives. Root
causes aren't going to make those choices for them.

In statements rationalizing their hatred of the United States,
Osama bin Laden and other advocates of radical Islamism have
cited U.S. foreign policy and its apparent disdain for the value of
Muslim lives. Poverty, oil, weapons, ideology, religious fanaticism,
and power underlie the situation they decry. And these factors
surely help to explain why so many people could be in a state of
frustrated resentment and could find it plausible to employ terrorist violence against Americans. In response to this situation, the

American people and their government may decide to change some policies while resolutely refusing to change others—and that's their responsibility. My own conviction is that it would be a profound mistake to keep issues of root causes out of public discussions—even granting that some resented elements involve commitments and values that one would not be willing to amend.

The point is, though, that root causes will never fully explain the choices and decisions of individuals. Why did Osama bin Laden, a millionaire many times over, go to Afghanistan to fight against the Soviet Union? Why did he devote enormous energy and personal resources to criticizing the Saudi government for its dependence on the United States? Use his considerable financial resources to fund radical Islamic groups in Sudan, Afghanistan, Pakistan, and elsewhere? Build elaborate terrorist training facilities in isolated caves in Afghanistan? There are thousands of Saudi millionaires whose background situations were similar in essence to bin Laden's and who made different life choices. This man could have ignored the poverty and humiliation of his fellow Muslims; he could have enjoyed a jet-setting life. Or he could have chosen to work nonviolently for the advancement of Muslim people by encouraging education, economic development, and the democratization of Muslim countries. He had choices; he made decisions. And for them he bears responsibility, as do others who have chosen to use violence as a political strategy.

Terrorist acts are the acts of persons who have chosen how to live in this world. We can refer to those choices in various ways. We can call chosen acts voluntary, or speak of free decisions, or free choices. Or we can say there is free will and these people are acting of their own free will. In legal talk, the standard term is *mens rea,* a Latin phrase meaning that the person has his or her mind on the thing and understands the nature of the act. In standard cases, *mens rea* is required for legal responsibility. There are many questions here and the details of moral and legal responsibility are debated. Insanity and mental incompetence, or being drugged or hypnotized, make for exceptions. Sometimes, important lines are hard to draw. But fundamentally, we accept that most of the time, most human agents are accountable for their actions. The existence of root causes does not deny the fact of choice. Many millions of people are poor and relatively powerless; some are doubtless frustrated and resentful; some of those are virulently anti-American. Of those, some train for terrorist action; and of those, some go on to commit terrorist acts. These men made their decisions, just as Osama bin Laden made his. Like him, they are responsible for their actions. Circumstances and "root causes" do not suffice to explain those actions because such factors do not explain the detailed choices of individual agents.

We can fully individualize, focus on the blameworthiness of perpetrators and the innocence of victims, and conclude that the explanation for terrorism must lie in the evil, wickedness, or insanity of particular individuals. That's a mistake. We can fully contextualize and think that there is an interplay of historical forces here and the whole explanation is to be found in root causes, in individual choices, and in actions emerging inevitably from broader social factors. That's a different mistake. What I'm suggesting is that if we avoid both of these mistakes, we can resolve the Antinomy of Terrorism. Kant proposed a solution to his antinomies by dissolving the contradictions apparently generated by his arguments. When you try to follow his account, you encounter all the apparatus of his metaphysics and theory of knowledge. I've avoided that apparatus here, but nevertheless, there's a fundamental sense in which my simpler theory copies that of Kant. It's based on a claim that causation and moral responsibility are compatible with each other and can exist together. Individuals are responsible for their actions and they make choices in contexts. To understand the choices, we need to understand the beliefs and motivations of individuals. To understand those contexts, we need to understand root causes. If we ever reached a complete understanding, it would fit both sorts of explanation together.

In the short term, we have to prevent individuals who have chosen terrorist affiliations from acting on their decisions to commit violent acts. In the long term, we have to reflect on the root causes of terrorism and address those we can, in keeping with our own values.

Notes

Archbishop Desmond Tutu's speech was given in Georgetown, Washington, D.C., and reported on the Internet through www.africana.com/news-home, October 31, 2001. My understanding of Osama bin Laden's life and attitudes owes much to Peter Bergen's *Holy War, Inc.: Inside the Secret World of Osama bin Laden* (New York: Free Press, 2001). The frustration and resentment felt by impoverished persons in the face of the affluence and power of the United States are movingly described by the Turkish writer Orhan Pamuk in "The Anger of the Damned," *New York Review of Books*, November 15, 2001. The lyrics for *West Side Story* were written by Stephen Sondheim. Kant's "Transcendental Dialectic" is the second part of his *Critique of Pure Reason*, trans. Norman Kemp Smith (New York: St. Martin's Press, 1965). The Antinomy of Causation and Freedom is the third of Kant's four antinomies. The belief that causation and free will can coexist is referred to as "compatibilism." Compatibilism is a theory favored by many philosophers and there are many versions of it. I claim no originality here, apart from the application of compatibilist ideas to the debate about the root causes of terrorism.

As of the winter of 2004, there is less resistance to the idea of seeking to understand the "root causes" of terrorism, but the debate between left and right with regard to responsibility issues is still conducted at a low level.

10

KINDNESS

Good can come of tragedy. On September 11, more than fifty planes landed in Gander, Newfoundland. Gander used to be a major refueling center for travel between North America and Europe, but now it is a small airport where few flights land on a normal day. On September 11, things were different. The town of 10,000 people was suddenly faced with the challenge of finding beds and food for some 6,500 people. People from churches, service clubs, shops, and medical centers acted immediately to host their unexpected and slightly bewildered visitors. There was a mass collection of food, some driven in from even smaller and more remote centers. Local inhabitants provided toothbrushes, soap, and other supplies, along with showers and, for many, guest bedrooms.

The small town of Lewisporte, some forty-five kilometers from Gander, hosted some 213 passengers from Delta Flight 15. Lewisporte is a small fishing village, and just about the whole town got involved in volunteering. The townspeople treated the anxious travelers as special guests, taking them on boat tours of the harbor and hikes in the woods. When the travelers were ready to leave three days later, they were so grateful they were in tears. Shirley Boothe-Jones was one of them. She and a fellow passenger wanted to "do something to thank these people." They decided to start a scholarship fund, and by the time their flight back to Cincinnati had landed, they had already collected some $14,000. In January, a television show about the project reported that $35,000 had been collected. The passengers on Delta 15 felt a powerful impulse to do something in return, to give back for what they had received, to reciprocate. The scholarship fund was a wonderful demonstration of the gratitude and affection they felt toward their generous hosts for hospitality spontaneously offered in a crisis. It's a tale worth the telling.

September 11 was the kind of day that makes people feel pessimistic about human nature. But killing and brutality were not the only things that happened that day. There were acts of striking courage and dedication on the part of rescue workers and others. And there were acts of generosity and kindness—people responding with energy and sympathy to strangers simply because they were people needing help. These were powerful testimonies to the human desire to help others. The other person does not have to be a relative, a friend, an acquaintance, or even a fellow countryman.

As a Canadian, I might try to claim some vicarious credit for the generosity of these Newfoundlanders who are my fellow citizens. Writing for the *New York Times,* one columnist said that the kindness and generosity were due to small-town values that didn't exist elsewhere in Canada. I wondered how she knew: had she carefully surveyed the rest of the country? But that's not the point, really. I don't think it's a question of contrasting small towns with big cities, or of contrasting Newfoundland with the rest of Canada, or Canada with the United States or some other country. This story is about human beings helping each other in a time of need. If I'm going to take vicarious credit for the energetic generosity of the folks in Lewisporte, I'd better do it on the grounds that I'm a human being. We human beings do things like this; there are countless tales about people showing kindness to strangers, and many of these instances occur in circumstances far more difficult than those of the Newfoundlanders on September 11. Another *New York Times* article told of "startling kindness" experienced by the writer when he was traveling in Afghanistan in the year 2000. A struggling man living in a brick hut offered the writer the family's last piece of bread, begging him to take it. The gesture was made from a sense of deeply felt obligation to extend hospitality to a stranger. Many cultures and peoples place enormous stress on values of hospitality and duties to offer food and drink to guests— even uninvited ones who come from afar.

Call it the ethic of hospitality. This ethic expresses a human impulse to sustain another human being in need. It is strong in many cultures, and I suspect it indicates feelings profoundly basic and important in human beings. I like to think that kind and generous acts arise from the sympathetic impulses we have because we are interdependent creatures. We have survived and continue to survive by cooperating with each other.

Writing in the eighteenth century, Adam Smith began his *Theory of the Moral Sentiments* with an account of the compassion human beings naturally feel for each other. Seeing suffering or pain, we imagine ourselves in the other's place and feel awful. Capitalists, take note. This is the same Adam Smith acclaimed for his theory of free market economics and for constructing the metaphor of an invisible hand. The invisible hand is a kind of underlying coordination that makes individual transactions, motivated by self-interest under conditions of market competition, work for the betterment of the whole of society. It's remarkable, to say the least, that the grand old man of market economics began his career as a moral philosopher who emphasized sentiments of compassion and sympathy. Speaking of human sympathy, Adam Smith said, "The greatest ruffian, the most hardened violator of the laws of society is not altogether without it." You might say that the invisible hand can operate only if it's wearing a moral glove, presumably also invisible. Adam Smith never stopped being a moral philosopher: He remained convinced that market economies require a moral foundation of honesty, promise keeping, trust, and reliable law. Without that basis, the pursuit of profit wouldn't provide an invisible hand; the result would be powerful thieves and the capitalism of brigands. Adam Smith believed that human nature makes ethics possible: Human beings can work within a moral framework because they naturally care what happens to each other—as the story of kindness in Lewisporte so powerfully illustrates.

Adam Smith's ideas were developed further by another Scottish philosopher of his time, David Hume. Hume put the point beautifully when he said, "Our minds are mirrors to one another." Being around a cheerful person tends to make us cheerful, but being around a depressed person tends to make us depressed. Citing these facts, Hume argued that the moods of other people affect us through the mechanism of sympathy. Because of our capacity for sympathy, we actually come to feel what others feel. Hume was an empiricist who believed that all our ideas come from sense experience. When we see another person sad or in trouble, we form an idea of his feelings and that idea becomes so powerful that it produces in us the very feeling itself. The modern expression "I feel for you" would have struck Hume as entirely apt; that's what he meant by sympathy. The impression of the other's suffering gives us such a vivid idea of feeling awful that we begin to suffer ourselves. Through our capacity for sympathy, we care what happens to other people; if we didn't care at all, customs and laws would count for nothing and we wouldn't bother to distinguish between useful practices and counterproductive ones. The other human being is a human being like us; we know that because we can feel it. If the other human being is a stranger, that makes no difference. The tendency to feel such sympathy is a fundamental part of our human constitution and a powerful element in what we feel and believe.

Hume and Adam Smith would have praised the people of Lewisporte—and everyone who extends hospitality to strangers and kindness to fellow human beings in need. But I don't think they would have been surprised by this heartfelt generosity. Both of them would have said, well, human nature is like that. It's a cheering thought in troubled times.

To act morally, we have to respect the interests and needs of other people. We can do this most easily if we are motivated to care what happens to other people. According to Hume and Adam Smith, our natural capacity for sympathy supports this motivation. It's important not to get this story backwards. Hume wasn't saying that we assist other people because we feel their pain and selfishly want to get rid of our own discomfort. That's not quite it. We want to make other people feel better because we care about them. That's what human sympathy is, and it's a ground-level fact of human life; we human beings really do care about each other. Dare I say it, we *naturally* care about each other.

A cynical observer might hypothesize hidden agendas among the good people of Newfoundland. Perhaps they assumed that many of the travelers they helped would be rich Americans and anticipated receiving something back from them: reputation, good connections, or money, for instance. A cynical interpreter can make any good news story look bleak. No real evidence is needed; he can just hypothesize a hidden agenda. Cynics can analyze everything from a negative point of view and make other people pretty depressed while they're at it. (The phenomenon confirms Hume's claim that depressed people tend to make others feel depressed.) But when cynical interpretations are based only on hypothesis and not on evidence, there's no good reason to take them seriously. The people who received this generous help in Newfoundland don't seem to have seen their generous hosts as self-serving, and strong friendships were formed in those few days after September 11. My sense is, it's good news; take it at face value, and don't let yourself be talked into believing that it has to mean something else. There are such things as human kindness and generosity, and believing in these things doesn't make you naïve or unsophisticated.

Not being cynically inclined myself, I return to the notion that human beings have a fundamental capacity for sympathy and that's why the suffering of other people affects us in the first place. I tend to agree with Hume and Adam Smith. Acts of generosity, heroism, and kindness have a source in our basic human makeup. That's why they can be found among people in all nations and cultures.

It was Alfred, Lord Tennyson, who wrote of "nature red in tooth and claw." As I understand the reference, Tennyson was referring to nonhuman animals in wild nature and to the killing that characterizes their struggle for life. Teeth, we've got, but human beings don't have claws: Tennyson wasn't saying that human nature was red in tooth and claw. In any event, if he had claimed that human nature was basically cruel, he would have been wrong. Kindness and generosity do not constitute evidence that some people successfully resist their real human impulses, those that would lead them to rape, pillage, and kill. For most of us, most of the time, such impulses don't have to be resisted. They don't exist.

Human nature has to provide for cooperation. If it didn't, our species never would have survived in the first place. It's an idea left unemphasized by theorists who write about the survival of the fittest and the selfish gene. But it is taken seriously by some anthropologists who argue that the deepest human need is for social bonding. One such account is offered by Mary E. Clark, who begins her argument by pointing out that human beings have large brains in proportion to the rest of their bodies. That means that human infants are born with relatively large heads and relatively helpless bodies, which in turn means that they need care over a long period of time. To provide that care, adults have to cooperate. Clark argues that the earliest human beings must have been creatures "programmed" to seek out and enjoy the company of their own kind; we are biologically constructed to trust one another and become members of intimate groups. As Clark would tell the human story, we are deeply social animals. Our struggle to survive involves interdependence, trust, and cooperation.

Is this too unscientific? Too simple and beautiful to be true? "Something's wrong with this picture," a cynic would say. And such is our exposure to deep and pervasive cynicism that we may readily follow the cynic's lead. What about the human penchant for brutality? Our notorious egoism? Our selfish nastiness? Our willingness to kill and maim each other in pursuit of our own goals? These aspects of human nature really exist and pose enormous problems. But they aren't the whole of human nature.

Acts of generosity and kindness are underrepresented in the news because they rarely pose problems. There's relatively little drama here: no scandal, no jeopardized careers, no blood and gore.

Which isn't to say that human nature is entirely good and wonderful. Nastiness persists in human beings, too. It's an undeniable fact that we can be deeply greedy and selfish, envious, despicable, and resentful. There are human beings who engage in killing on a grand scale, some showing hardly a twinge of conscience, a few even taking malicious delight. If we reflect on this, it makes for a bleak picture—as journalists and theorists frequently remind us.

Yes, human beings want power. But even power requires relationships with other people and, besides, it's not the only thing we want. We also seek such things as knowledge, a sense of worth and achievement, and happiness—all of which require decent relationships with other people. We care about other people—how they are faring and how they respond to us. Our own happiness depends on theirs; and theirs depends on ours. We want to connect with them and have them want to connect with us. Moving stories about care for strangers illustrate these basic facts about human nature. The people in Gander and Lewisporte, Newfoundland, behaved with energy and generosity, and they were wonderful in a crisis, which is good news. And we should appreciate good news when we hear it. But there's even better news: Those capacities for sympathy and kindness are shared by human beings everywhere.

Notes

My account of the events in Gander and Lewisporte draws on Margaret Wente's "Cruel Hoaxes and the Kindness of Strangers," *Globe and Mail,* October 27, 2001; and Barbara Crossette's "Unexpected Guests Warm Hearts in the Frozen North," *New York Times,* November 18, 2001. The story of hospitality in Afghanistan is taken from Dexter Filkins, "In a Wasteland, Casual Brutality and Acts of Startling Kindness," *New York Times,* November 18, 2001. Comments about Adam Smith on sympathy are based on *The Theory of Moral Sentiments,* as excerpted in L. A. Selby-Bigge, ed., *British Moralists* (Indianapolis: Bobbs-Merrill, 1964). Hume's comments on sympathy appear throughout his *Treatise of Human Nature,* ed. L. A. Selby-Bigge (Oxford: Clarendon Press, 1965). Tennyson's phrase "Nature red in tooth and claw" occurs in his poem, "In Memoriam." An explanation of Mary E. Clark's anthropological theory can be found in her article, "Meaningful Social Bonding as a Universal Human Need," in *Conflict: Human Needs Theory,* ed. John Burton (New York: St. Martin's Press, 1990).

11

COURAGE

The September 11 attacks inspired an interesting debate about courage. President George W. Bush said the attacks were the acts of "faceless cowards." A few rare spirits, Bill Maher and Susan Sontag among them, were brave enough to question the epithet, and made themselves highly unpopular for doing so. Obviously President Bush thought the attacks were morally appalling and used the word "cowards" to express strong moral criticism. Maher and Sontag were probably imagining how it would feel to deliberately fly a large plane into a skyscraper, knowing that in doing so one would go straight to a fiery death. Surely that would take nerve; so whatever else might be said about the hijackers, they weren't cowards.

Courageous people can persist in pursuing their goals despite physical dangers, but this is not to say that they have no fear or are unaware of the risks. Courage is not the same as fearlessness. You may be fearless because you are rash or unaware of dangers, which would mean that you act boldly; but your boldness wouldn't amount to courage. What's needed for courage is an ability to manage and persist even in the face of realistic fears. The eighteenth-century essayist Samuel Johnson said, "Courage is a quality so necessary for maintaining virtue, that it is always respected, even when it is associated with vice." What Johnson meant, I think, is that without courage a person cannot consistently exercise any other virtue. If you are afraid of physical hazards or social disapproval, there will be occasions when fears will prevent you from acting on your other good qualities—honesty, loyalty, intelligence, or whatever else they might be. Johnson was thinking of courage as a sort of second-level quality, a virtue that we need if we want to exercise other virtues reliably.

The dispute about the courage of suicide attackers illustrates what has been called "the politics of courage." Because the word "courage" functions as a term of praise, we don't want to apply it to someone whose actions we profoundly disapprove of—even if that person does show physical daring and persistence in the face of danger. If we're against burglary, we won't want to say that a burglar who crossed a shaky plank to reach a safe showed courage in doing so. And if we're against turning civilian aircraft into weapons of mass destruction, we won't want to say that the September 11 attackers showed courage. That's what underlies President Bush's comment. Similarly, the Japanese kamikaze pilots who knowingly went to their deaths in bombing Pearl Harbor were deemed by Western commentators to be fanatical, not courageous.

Yet Sontag and Maher obviously have a point. The September 11 attackers clearly did have the ability to persist towards their goals in the face of dangerous obstacles. They knowingly took the ultimate risk and exposed themselves to certain death.

Here's the problem. If courage is a virtue, we don't want to allow that people have it when they are pursuing bad ends. But if courage is a second-level virtue, it is displayed in the exercise of other qualities of character, and that would include bad qualities as well as good ones.

In ancient Greece, discussions of courage raised questions about knowledge: the knowledge of dangers, and also knowledge about which goals were worth pursuing, and why. In Plato's dialogue *Laches*, Socrates and Laches arrive at the idea that only wise endurance can be courage, so courage requires knowledge about what must be done. But then they struggle to differentiate between courage and knowledge. Aristotle had the same idea: He said that courage, like other virtues, requires wisdom and a balance of reason and passion in persisting toward one's goal. Courage requires a sensible balance, a kind of golden mean between fear and confidence. A courageous person is good at facing fears and can expose himself or herself to hazards, and even to death if that's what is necessary to pursue valuable and reasonable goals. Given the *good reasons* that are needed, moral understanding enters the picture; therefore, like Plato, Aristotle wouldn't be willing to say that a person displays courage when he is pursuing a bad end. This being so, Aristotle would have supported the comments of the president. Since killing thousands of people and devastating a city and economy are bad ends, and bad ends cannot be endorsed for good reasons, the hijackers couldn't have acted for good reason; thus they shouldn't be credited with the virtue of courage. If we adopt Aristotle's approach, we will never allow that anyone attacking us or putting himself in the role of our enemy has courage, because we will never accept the enemy's goals as worthy of pursuit. Playing the politics of courage is unobjectionable, from this point of view. Bad ends can't be pursued for good reasons and courage is related to knowledge in such a way that it requires acting for good reasons.

A perplexing feature of this position is that it seems to ignore the descriptive content of the word "courage," linking it with an ability to act even where fear would be warranted. And it doesn't fit with the role of courage as a second-level virtue. It seems rather arrogant. Is it only the "right people"—those people who agree with us—who can be courageous? Couldn't we sometimes allow courage to our enemies? Winston Churchill once faced this question. On October 14, 1939, a German naval officer, Gunther Prien, was commanding the sub U-47, which penetrated a heavily defended harbor where the British fleet was anchored. Prien and his men managed to sink a 29,150-ton battleship, the HMS *Royal*

Oak. The attack cost 830 British lives. Prien and his crew were not suicide attackers; in fact, all escaped without injury. When they returned to Germany, they were celebrated as heroes. Obviously, Churchill was not happy about these actions because they were disastrous from the British point of view. Nevertheless, he was willing to grant that Prien and his men had shown courage, even though they were soldiers in a Nazi navy reporting to Adolf Hitler. Churchill allowed that theirs was "a remarkable exploit of skill and daring."

Prien was an enemy of Britain, just as the September 11 hijackers were enemies of the United States. There are differences, of course; Prien's actions were undertaken when the two states, Britain and Germany, were officially at war with each other, whereas the acts of September 11 were surprise attacks launched by clandestine agents in what was officially a time of peace. And Prien and his men were not suicide attackers, which marks another key difference. The fear that people face in contexts of courage is most obviously the fear of physical dangers, and most thinking about courage assumes that the ultimate physical harm that a person can suffer is his or her own death. Suicide attackers not only tolerate a risk of death but also walk straight into it, deliberately ending their own lives to wreak death and destruction on others. Does it follow from their willingness to incur their own deaths that suicide attackers are especially courageous?

The question is puzzling. There seems to be a sense in which these attackers and other "Islamic martyrs" don't truly believe that they will die. If they don't think they are going to die because they assume they are going straight from this world into another one, they have nothing to fear; therefore they have no fear to overcome and no need for courage. Apparently, al-Qaeda recruitment materials from bin Laden promised that death would be no more than a "pinch," and right after the pinch, these "martyrs" in the cause of pure Islam would go straight to paradise. These men apparently thought of themselves as being in transition to a place far better than this world; in this heaven they would experience wonderful pleasures—including, significantly, lots of sex. A letter found in the baggage of Mohamed Atta, the leader of the September 11 group, spoke of going through the gates of Paradise to encounter seventy-two virgins and experience sexual ecstasy. It's hard for the secular mind to contemplate such a full and literal belief in an afterworld, but if the fiery death is truly understood as a trivially painful moment marking the entrance to Paradise, there should have been no fear. The death of one's physical body would be desired; arguably, on such a hypothesis, one's death would not occur at all. Such reasoning about death, immortality, and fear could support President Bush's comments—though I doubt he had anything like this in mind.

Physical courage is what we're thinking about in these contexts, and when we think of physical courage, it tends to be the battle-field that first comes to mind. We assume there is fear to be overcome and it's fear of one's own death, and there's a goal to be pursued and it's victory for one's own group. The paradigm of physical courage is that of the brave soldier risking his life to defend his country. Of course, physical courage is not needed only in times of war. Firefighters, rescue workers, and police officers need it too, and can display it mightily, as so many heroically did on September 11.

William Miller is the author of a widely read recent book on courage. His interest in courage arose from his fascination with Icelandic sagas, tales of war and vengeance in an ancient honor culture. A wiry, muscular chap and a highly aggressive speaker, Miller portrays courage as a masculine virtue. As he understands it, with courage come war, strife, and a theory of manhood; Miller acknowledges moral courage, but not with any great enthusiasm. When I met Miller, I found myself wanting to resist his assumption that courage was something best exhibited by men in conflict. I was far more interested in the kind of moral courage displayed by those who risk social ostracism, a bad reputation, loss of a job, or some other social loss by standing up for what they think is right. Someone who is a whistleblower, exposing incompetence or corruption in an organization in which he is employed, shows moral courage. Typically the risks are social; though in extreme cases, unpopularity brings physical risks as well.

When the struggle against terrorism began in earnest, it took moral courage to criticize the use of physical force in response. Public opinion was so strongly behind the military campaign that voices of dissent were unwelcome. Barbara Lee, a Democrat from the Bay Area in San Francisco, opposed congressional authorization of the use of force and was the only person in Congress to do so. Friends had warned her against the move, saying, "You don't want to be out there alone." After the vote, Lee received thousands of harsh messages and needed police protection. Taking this stance took considerable moral courage. Moral courage is linked to physical courage, which we can understand when we reflect on Barbara Lee's need of police protection after the vote. If you become sufficiently unpopular, you may actually be exposing yourself to physical risks: someone might set fire to your house or assault you in the street, or you might be taken in by the authorities on the grounds that you were a terrorist sympathizer and kept for months in detention without access to your family or to legal assistance. The basis of courage is the ability to expose ourselves knowingly and sensibly to risks in pursuit of our goals. Physical courage obviously requires this ability and, given the implications of standing up for unpopular causes, moral courage often requires it too.

Most people think of Socrates as someone who displayed moral courage because he stood up for independent thought and the right to speak out at his trial in Athens in 399 B.C.E. He was not intimidated by the thought that he would be sentenced to death for speaking his mind. After his sentence, Socrates sat in a prison cell for a month while he awaited his death by poison; during this time, he was calm and cheerful, reassuring his friends and conducting discussions of themes such as immortality and the nature of the soul. For author William Miller, it's not this moral courage that is fundamentally interesting about Socrates. Miller glorifies physical courage in times of war, and for him the profoundly important point about Socrates is that he had been a war hero. This man was not a philosopher like the others. He was no weakly intellectual but rather a sturdy chap, broad and tough and strong, capable of standing for hours barefoot on ice and renowned for his bravery and endurance in battle. Socrates had demonstrated his physical courage fighting for Athens. His moral courage and his physical courage were both premised on his willingness to expose himself to physical death.

When I studied Miller's book in preparation for a panel discussion, I found myself wanting to engage with him in "the politics of courage." I admire Socrates for his moral courage and his questioning and take little interest in his having been a good soldier. I wanted to resist the paradigm of the masculine war hero that was implicit in so much of Miller's discussion. Hundreds of examples over hundreds of pages told of men in battle, physically contending with each other to prove their honor or defend their country. Avenging insults and wrongs was assumed to be good, and old "honor" cultures, along with their feuds and vendettas, were exalted in an ongoing narrative of male heroism, battle, killing, and death. The militarism bothered me. And so did the tacky antifeminism that often accompanied it. In the days of Icelandic sagas, men who weren't deemed courageous by their peers were called "girls" or "women." Miller quoted such language repeatedly, and with apparent approval; he seemed oblivious to the reality that, in giving birth, women need considerable courage and fortitude.

I can understand that for men in war the issue of courage is profoundly important and challenging. As long as there are wars, some people will need to fight in them; some of these people will need to display courage in doing so; and historically, nearly all of these people have been men. But the discussions of honor and fighting and revenge and being manly left me craving examples of moral courage from civilian life—people who showed courage in whistle-blowing, or facing harassment or job loss for championing some important but popularly resisted cause.

On December 6, 2001, I had the good fortune to hear a lecture by Sima Samar, an Afghani physician. Samar had received a substantial human rights award and was on a lecture tour as a result. By coincidence, the previous day, she had been appointed to the cabinet of the provisional government in Afghanistan. She would be one of two women and one of five deputy prime ministers in the new government. Samar is a founder of the Shuhada organization, a group that managed against enormous obstacles to found schools, health clinics, and hospitals in Afghanistan and neighboring regions of Pakistan. Shuhada institutions served men and women, boys and girls, contrary to Taliban policies in Afghanistan. Even though some facilities were bombed by Taliban forces and some staff were killed, the organization kept its hospitals and clinics open in the period between 1996 and 2001. A preliminary description of Samar's courageous work in an introduction so impressed the audience that she was given a standing ovation before she spoke.

Samar identified education as the most important goal for the rebuilding of her country. Under the Taliban, Afghanistan had been in the power of men of extremely limited education. Many officials in the government were illiterate. She described a telling encounter with a United Nations development officer in 1989. At that point, the Afghani and foreign *mujahadeen* had succeeded in driving the Soviets out of Afghanistan and Islamic fundamentalism had gained enormous power because of its anti-Soviet credentials.

Samar asked the UN official whether there were development plans involving women in any way. Taken aback, the official told her frankly that the UN had not taken women into account and had no plans for development that involved women. He said that he had not even seen any women in Afghanistan. Surely there were no women there. Samar pointed out that she was an Afghani woman, and he was seeing her, after all, so he had seen at least one Afghani woman. The official replied that he found it difficult to believe she was Afghani; she had green eyes. "These men have to come from somewhere," she pointed out. No society can persist without women, and plans for development that omitted more than half the population were doomed to failure. The official acknowledged her point, but nothing was done about it.

Another Afghani feminist, Soraya Parlika, helped to organize a network of secret schools for girls in Kabul during the Taliban period. One course cost $1 per month; women and girls went about hiding books under their burqas and risking their safety to study math, computing, and English. This was courage.

In areas where the Taliban were not fully in control, it was easier to operate Shuhada schools, which provided for some 20,000 students. The schools were primitive, Samar said. Usually, the children just sat on mud. They were so pleased to come to school that many walked as long as three hours to get there, often with no shoes. These walks must have taken a lot of endurance—and bravery too, given the possibility of detection by the Taliban and the numerous land mines that could kill or maim at any time.

Describing her activities, Samar said that she had encountered considerable opposition from the antifemale Taliban; but eventually, "I was able to impose myself upon them." This suggestive comment left me craving the details. She was a small woman, rather slim, and I should have loved to know more about how this "imposition" worked. Obviously, her influence could not have been due to physical force; she must have possessed considerable negotiating skills. Perhaps the Taliban needed doctors, even female ones, to treat their wounded, and such needs had given her negotiating power. Probably her enormous moral energy had made itself felt, even in these extraordinary circumstances.

My sense is that our times call for more moral courage, and many of the people who are exhibiting it in their daily lives are anything but well-known heroes. Some of the elements of military courage strike me as dangerous: the potent ego, the bold risk, the heroic struggle against the hated enemy, the great adventure, the meaning found in violent struggle—not to mention the misogynism that so readily accompanies all this.

Some fifteen years before the September 11 attacks, Amelie Rorty wrote a thoughtful essay about the virtue of courage. In the aftermath of the attacks, one of her themes haunts me. Rorty suggested that we tend to interpret the world in ways that provide opportunities for us to exercise those virtues and capacities that we possess. We are drawn to situations in which we can display what we think is best about ourselves. Here's my application of her idea to the present situation. If we value physical courage, believe we possess it, and have a battlefield paradigm of what courage is, we will tend to interpret the world as a place full of dangerous physical challenges, to which we can respond. Because we will devote our resources to meeting those sorts of challenges, we will cultivate military hardware and personnel as distinct from institutions for negotiation, mediation, law, education, and social development. We will be drawn to meet physical challenges; while doing so, we will expect to show our bravery and prowess and to use the capacities we have developed. It's a little bit like the old adage "If your only tool is a hammer, all the world's a nail." To be sure, physical courage is valuable and necessary. But as the ancients knew, it has to be kept in its proper place.

Notes

The example of Gunther Prien comes from Douglas Walton's essay, "Courage, Relativism and Practical Reasoning," *Philosophia*, 20, (Israel, 1990–1992), 227–239. An account of Aristotle's ideas about courage may be found in Anthony Duff, "Aristotelian Courage," *Ratio*, 29, (1987), 2–15. Plato discussed courage in his dialogue *Laches*, in which Socrates is the main character; a translation of this dialogue by Benjamin Jowett appears in Edith Hamilton and Huntingdon Cairns, *Plato: Collected Dialogues* (New York: Bollingden Foundation, Pantheon Books, 1961). William Miller's book, *The Mystery of Courage*, was published by Harvard University Press in 2000. I met Miller in May 2001 when I participated in a panel discussion of his work sponsored by the Canadian Association of University Teachers of Law and held in Quebec City. Dr. Sima Samar's talk was given at the University of Calgary in December 6, 2001. The case of Barbara Lee is explained in *The Nation* for October 8, 2001. Soraya Parlika's activities were described in *Time Magazine* for December 3, 2001. Amelie Rorty's essay, "Two Faces of Courage," appeared in *Philosophy*, 61, (1986): 151–171.

Sima Samar held two positions in Afghanistan's interim government under Hamid Karzai: those of deputy prime minister and minister for women's affairs. In June 2002, she resigned those positions due to threats against her life by Muslim fundamentalists who claimed that she was not a Muslim, renounced *Sharia* law, and was "the Salman Rushdie of Islam." Afghanistan's superior court dismissed the charges, which were apparently based on an erroneous account in a Canadian newspaper. Karzai immediately appointed Samar Afghanistan's Independent Commissioner for Human Rights, a position she still occupies. Samar speaks indefatiguably to urge the importance of severe problems in her country, decrying the power of warlords and continuing attacks by Taliban, al Qaeda, and others against women and girls. As of 2003, some thirty girls' schools have been destroyed by fundamentalists, and women in some areas were immolating themselves to avoid forced marriages. A journalist who visited Samar's office reported that it was guarded by men with Kalashnikovs.

In January, 2004, an Afghanistan constitution was agreed upon. It guarantees equal rights and duties to men and women, calls for at least two female delegates from each province, and requires 50% of all presidential appointments to the House of Elders to be women. The constitution stipulates that Afghanistan will abide by the U.N. Charter and other international treaties, including the U.N. Declaration of Human Rights. However, in the context of warlordism and continuing violence, such provisions will be hard to enforce. In addition, there is a provision that no law can be contrary to the beliefs and provisions of "the sacred religion of Islam," and this provision is worrisome to some observers, including those concerned about the position of women.

12

PERSPECTIVE

In his essay "On Liberty," John Stuart Mill offered a strong defense of the freedom of discussion. Whether an opinion is true or false, Mill said, it is a profound mistake to prevent its dissemination. If we suppress an opinion that is true, we deprive ourselves of the chance to learn the truth. If we suppress an opinion that is false, we deprive ourselves of the chance to appreciate the truth more fully. Beliefs unsupported by reasons are no better than superstitions, and it is the exposure of beliefs to criticism that best allows us to understand the reasons for them. "He who knows only his own side of the case knows little of that," said Mill. I'm tempted to add another line of thought to Mill's argument: If we don't know whether an opinion is true or false, the best way to find out is to engage in public investigation and debate.

Mill emphasized the fact of human fallibility. To put it bluntly, we all make mistakes. And it's more than an individual matter: Groups and nations, ages and cultures are fallible, too. Mill is not arguing for total skepticism. He doesn't say we should hold back from believing or refuse to make commitments based on our beliefs. It wouldn't be possible, anyway; we have to act, and our beliefs provide the basis for our actions. But the fact that we rely on our beliefs is no justification for suppressing dissent. Even if we're utterly confident that what we believe is correct, we should allow other people to express their opinions and make arguments for them. It's the only way to correct errors, amend our judgments, and support our confidence with reasons. The strength of human judgment is that it can be set right when it is wrong, Mill says, criticizing people in his own time who were convinced their opinions were indispensable but unconcerned about their truth.

If people are forbidden from disagreeing with orthodoxy, orthodoxy will be established as dogma. This is the way for societies to make mistakes, often big ones. When large complex societies encounter multifaceted problems, their capacity to make ramified mistakes is vast—which makes Mill's nineteenth-century arguments all the more important today. The notion that because there is a crisis everyone should rally together and agree is exactly backwards: we may be rallying to support mistaken ideas and in doing so depriving ourselves of a chance to find our mistakes. Or so Mill would have argued—and I think he's right.

In traditions stemming back before John Stuart Mill to the French Revolution, and earlier, most people in Western countries have enjoyed freedom of speech and freedom of conscience. Constitutional provisions and bills of rights entrench these values, and public rhetoric usually exalts them. However, our commitment tends to waver in difficult circumstances. Once the United States and its allies had committed themselves to a war against terrorism, dissent became difficult and highly unpopular. A California professor who criticized the media coverage of Muslims in a panel discussion told me how she was criticized by a chief of police. He told her firmly that because it was a time of war, she should keep her opinions to herself. In war, there is no room for dissent.

I don't agree. I'm convinced that the struggle against terrorism more than permits disagreement and debate; it actually requires them. It's not because individuals possess rights to free speech, though such rights are significant and valuable. Nor is the need for dissent based on an ethic of tolerance—although that's important too. The point is rather different; it's a matter of real social need. We need careful thinking and a thorough exploration of the issues, and we aren't going to get it if all the people who think in unorthodox ways are intimidated into silence. We can best understand our situations by exploring diverse accounts, reasons and evidence, arguments and counterarguments about them. Only through a public critical discussion of various theories and arguments can we expose errors, correct omissions, understand or amend our values, and arrive at fresh insights and novel hypotheses. This is no time to silence people because they are Muslims or pacifists or foreigners, or because we ourselves feel so vulnerable that we can't bear to be questioned.

With these themes in mind, let's consider some unpopular theories about September 11 and the war against terrorism. Differing from orthodox accounts, they haven't figured much in mainstream media and debate.

Theory One: Jews plotted attacks against the World Trade Center and the Pentagon and carried them out, arranging things so that it would look as though Muslim men had hijacked the planes. Because Jews who worked in the World Trade Center were warned in advance of the attacks, none of them died. The motivation underlying the alleged Jewish plot was to strengthen U.S. support for Israel. Apparently many in the Muslim world continue to believe this theory even after viewing several videos in which Osama bin Laden virtually admitted responsibility for the attacks. Call this the Theory of Zion.

The Theory of Zion is wildly implausible and the key premise cited in its support is simply false. Many Jews went to work at the World Trade Center on September 11, and many were killed in the attacks. The Theory of Zion presumes that the Israelis find such an enormous gap in the support they are getting from the United States that they would undertake an extraordinarily risky and destabilizing action in an attempt to buttress that support. It also assumes many other highly implausible things—for instance, that it would be possible to put nineteen people of Islamic background on the hijacked flights and arrange that those people would appear to passengers to be the hijackers, even though they were not. It presumes either that Osama bin Laden himself was complicit with Jews or that videotaped statements in which he took pride in the attacks were faked by Israeli agents.

The Theory of Zion is inspired in part by the deep conviction that killing thousands of civilians is so seriously and clearly wrong that no Muslim could do it. Another motivating factor is suspicion of Jews so strong as to merit the name of anti-Semitism.

Theory Two: People in the CIA and the FBI knew that bin Laden and his al-Qaeda collaborators were planning these attacks. They knew because they had received many warnings in advance—various anonymous tips, and warnings from German and Russian intelligence. Had they sought to, they could have prevented the attacks; since they didn't prevent them, we can infer that they didn't try. And there's a motive that will make sense of this stunning omission: agents in the CIA and FBI had reasons of their own for wanting these attacks to occur. If the American people saw the country attacked by terrorists, they would support an expansive military campaign enhancing the resources and power of the military. The resulting realignment of U.S. policy would favor oil interests, militarism, and U.S. domination around the world. The war against terrorism has indeed resulted in tremendous public support for the U.S. military campaign. Thus, it's argued, the attacks must have been sponsored or tolerated by people who were working from inside government agencies to build that public support. Call this the Theory of Internal Collusion.

Sources available through the Internet cite arguments in favor of the Theory of Internal Collusion. One such argument is based on the tragic story of John O'Neill. O'Neill left his position as deputy director of the FBI in August 2001 to become chief of security at the World Trade Center. On September 11, he entered the second tower just after it was attacked. He died while attempting to assist other people. Authors Charles Brisard and Guillaume Dasquie tell O'Neill's story in a recent book and argue that it was frustration with internal obstacles to his investigations into al-Qaeda terrorism that led O'Neill to leave his post with the FBI. Brisard and Dasquie maintain that O'Neill complained to them that the U.S. State Department had blocked his attempts to prove bin Laden's guilt in such key events as the 1993 bombing of the World Trade Center; the 1996 bombing of a U.S. base in Saudi Arabia; the 1998 bombings of U.S. embassies in Nairobi and Dar Es Salaam; and the 2000 bombing of the USS *Cole*.

Another argument for the Theory of Internal Collusion is based on the claim that while Osama bin Laden was a patient undergoing treatment for a chronic kidney infection at a Dubai hospital in July 2001, he was visited by a top CIA official in his private suite. The story is cited as having appeared in *Le Figaro* on October 31, 2001; *Le Figaro* cited hospital staff in Dubai as confirming that bin Laden had been there. But on November 1 of the same year, the Ananova News Agency reported that the staff in Dubai denied any such thing.

There is also an allegation based on timing. Why was President George W. Bush not informed about the September 11 attacks until more than an hour after the first hijacking occurred? This delay, it's said, meant that air force planes were not ordered to intercept the hijacked planes until more than seventy-five minutes after the first hijacking, at which point it was too late. Advocates of Internal Collusion allege that the attacks were a setup and attribute the delay to deliberate obstruction by persons seeking to advance their own agenda by collaborating with bin Laden.

Were the attacks a setup? I doubt it. The idea that U.S. intelligence operatives would collude in such devastating attacks against their own country, including such potent symbols as the World

Trade Center and the Pentagon, strikes me as wildly unlikely. To make such hypotheses credible, highly compelling arguments would be required. And the arguments put forward aren't compelling. Take the matter of unheeded warnings. Because intelligence agencies get thousands of warnings about possible attacks, they can't know for certain which ones to take seriously. A clue that is highly significant after an event might not have seemed significant or reliable when it was first noted. Huge amounts of barely organized prior information may not add up to what, with hindsight, can be seen to be the correct conclusion. Relevant here is the stock saying that hindsight gives twenty-twenty vision. Poor coordination between agencies, the weight of too much information, overwork, carelessness, and just plain stupidity can readily explain omissions and misinterpretations. We don't need to appeal to a conspiracy theory.

As regards the narrative of John O'Neill, for all his brilliance and hard-driving dedication, it appears that John O'Neill was a difficult personality. In some colleagues, he inspired intense loyalty; in others, considerable animosity. Some found O'Neill obsessive; to them his "fixation" with anti-American terrorism seemed unbalanced. His personal life was highly complex; he had an estranged wife from whom he was not divorced and two serious women friends, both of whom he apparently wanted to marry. One lived in New York, giving him a powerful reason to accept a job there. O'Neill had moments of absentmindedness: once, when he left a meeting to make a phone call, he left unattended a briefcase containing important documents. The briefcase was stolen, resulting in a serious security breach. O'Neill's failure to advance his agenda at the FBI before September 11 could have had many causes; that failure doesn't prove that bin Laden sympathizers in the FBI or the CIA were conspiring against him.

Concerning the Dubai hospital, the report that Osama bin Laden received visitors there is contested, so the story alleging CIA involvement with his plans for September 11 is an uncertain basis for allegations against the CIA. Now what about the argument about timing problems? Is collusion with the hijackers the most likely hypothesis to explain delayed communications on September 11? I don't think so. There are other possible, and more plausible, explanations: panic, bureaucratic muddles, and confusion about authority being obvious contenders.

To say the least, there are some questionable logical inferences in the arguments offered to support the Theory of Internal Collusion. Basically, its theme is that there are some little-known facts that the standard theory can't explain and that the Internal Collusion theory can explain, so the Internal Collusion theory must be true. This line of reasoning is a caricature of a recognized form of argument known as "inference to the best explanation." As its name would suggest, for such an argument to be used properly, the inferred explanation must be the *best* of those proposed. It's a requirement that raises the awkward logical question as to what makes an explanation *best*, and that question is not so easy to answer. But one thing is clearly necessary for a proposed explanation to be a good one: The inferred hypothesis has to cohere with relevant background knowledge; it has to be plausible in the light of other beliefs that have been deemed plausible or true. If you think of O'Neill's story in the light of the requirement, you can see the problem. What's more plausible—that U.S. intelligence agents engaged in professional rivalries and turf wars, or that some of them colluded with anti-American terrorists to permit devastating al-Qaeda attacks on the United States? The first hypothesis involves several well-known features of human beings working together in bureaucracies. The second, on the other hand, is highly improbable. So the argument doesn't work, and O'Neill's tragic story doesn't provide good reasons for believing in the Theory of Internal Collusion.

Theory Three: The September 11 attacks were a case of "the chickens coming home to roost." U.S. foreign policy has for many decades inspired resentment around the world, and its wealth and power have inspired envy. Among millions of people, anti-Americanism has been rampant, even virulent. Poor and oppressed people, frustrated with circumstances in their own countries, and tired of living under elitist governments backed up by U.S. power, march by the millions, yelling "Death to America." The arrogance and insensitivity of the United States, the widely broadcast affluence of many of its people, and its status as the one remaining super-armed superpower, ready and willing to bully its way around the world in general and the Middle East in particular, were inevitably going to bring this kind of result. Especially significant are intense opposition in the Muslim world to U.S. support for Israel, the stationing of U.S. troops in Saudi Arabia, and the effects of prolonged sanctions against Iraq. September 11, 2001, was the inevitable culmination of all this anti-Americanism. It was the day the chickens came home to roost. Call this the Theory of Roosting Chickens.

Unlike the Theories of Zion and Internal Collusion, this theory is not primarily about what caused the attacks. Fundamentally, it is a moral analysis of U.S. foreign policy itself. Based on a critique of that policy, it sees resentment of the United States as inevitable and traces responsibility for the attacks through that resentment to the United States itself.

But whatever the rights and wrongs of American attitudes, culture, and foreign policy, the Theory of Roosting Chickens seems grounded on an overly simplistic understanding of responsibility. The problem lies in the implication underlying this theory, its notion that if foreign policy is objectionable, those who have supported that foreign policy become morally responsible for attacks against themselves. Although it is surely true that U.S. foreign policy merits reexamination, the Roosting Chickens theory confuses some of many root causes of terrorism with the individual responsibility that comes from decision and choice. It is also open to criticism on the grounds that it fails to acknowledge reasons that might support U.S. foreign policy. The Theory of Roosting Chickens amounts, in effect, to a reversed double standard. A common mistake in situations of conflict is Our Side Bias in interpreting and evaluating information; obviously such bias will lead to errors and we should try to avoid it. But we will also make mistakes if we systematically favor the other side and adopt Their Side Bias, reversing the common mistake. And advocates of the Theory of Roosting Chickens seem to reason in this way by blaming U.S. foreign policy for these attacks while failing to criticize the radical Islamist terrorists who planned them and carried them out. They ignore some obvious truths: radical Islamists have a violent, simplistic, and radically misogynistic view of the world and are taking an unreasonable stance in blaming the United States for all that's wrong in the Muslim world. Their simplistic blaming of outsiders ignores long-standing attitudes and beliefs inhibiting development, science, and democracy in Muslim countries—highly significant among these being the oppression of women and the absence of traditions of critical thinking and scientific inquiry. Blaming the United States also ignores a fundamental fact about imperialist exploitation; such an exercise of power is possible only when there is effective consent on the part of those exploited.

   Theory Four: The September 11 attacks were terrorist attacks planned and carried out by members of the al-Qaeda network under the inspiration and leadership of Osama bin Laden. The attacks were clearly wrong, killed thousands of innocent people, and did enormous damage to the United States and other countries. The United States had to respond effectively to those attacks, to protect its interests and prevent further terrorist attacks. To do so, it needed the cooperation of the international community. Highly relevant matters were better immigration, visa, and passport controls, coordinated police work, and stricter attention to financial networks supplying money to terrorist groups and supporters. The situation was indeed one in which there was a general terrorist threat, and that threat called for a focused response by the United States and the international community. But it did not require a *military* response by the United States and associated countries. It did not require, or justify, the bombing of Afghanistan and the killing of Afghan civilians who were innocent bystanders no more responsible for the attacks than those killed in the United States.

The United States could have sought the cooperation of the international community to further isolate the Taliban regime and persuade it to hand over bin Laden and other al-Qaeda leaders. Those persons arrested could have been submitted to the appropriate international authorities and put on trial for their criminal activities in an appropriate court; this could have been either an international tribunal established under the auspices of the United Nations or another court recognized in the international community as observing due legal process and having the capacity to try the accused fairly and impartially. A nonviolent response would have been possible. Call this the Gandhian Internationalist Theory.

This is where my heart is—with Gandhi and the internationalists. I have a lot of sympathy for this theory. I find little evidence that it was taken seriously by the powers that be, and I deeply regret that. I believe the United States should have negotiated with the Taliban regime in September at the point when it was asking for evidence linking Osama bin Laden with the attacks of September 11. In rejecting outright such negotiations, the U.S. administration lost any claim to have seriously explored all the nonviolent alternatives to bombing Afghanistan and thus all claim that it was fighting a just war. Resorting to loose rhetoric about bringing people to justice without taking seriously the issue of appropriate legal tribunals betrayed a cavalier attitude to the rule of law. Predictably, the actions of the administration led to the questionable treatment of men taken prisoner and resulted in a considerable loss of moral credibility for the United States. A genuinely internationalist approach at this point would have been far better. The failure to take nonviolent options and international institutions seriously is due, I think, to a deep and uncritical bias in favor of military responses to conflict and a tragic unreflective pessimism about the possibilities of well-developed and well-funded international institutions. I'm convinced that if even a modest portion of the vast sums allocated to military equipment were devoted to the development of international institutions of law, violence prevention, conflict resolution, education, and development, most political conflicts could be addressed with a level of violence far lower than we normally presume. There's a vicious circle in so much of our thinking. We assume that military force is a solution, and the only solution; and by that very assumption we fail to develop alternative institutions and strategies that would make constructive nonviolent interventions possible.

But for all my deep sympathies, I have to confess to some doubts about the response to the September 11 attacks in particular. My very reluctant skepticism is based on my sense that, in this context, the Gandhian Internationalist Theory requires us to assume too many doubtful hypothetical claims. Even if the U.S. administration had negotiated with the Taliban, I doubt that they would have agreed to hand over bin Laden and his cohorts. The Taliban saw these people as "guests" and were highly sympathetic to their ideology; even more relevantly, the Taliban were heavily dependent on al-Qaeda for military and financial support. And even in the unlikely event that they would have been willing to hand over bin Laden and thousands of fighters, it's doubtful whether they had sufficient control of Afghanistan to do so. And as for international legal authority, while I greatly favor its development, the problem is that there are no police to enforce international law. Even presuming that negotiations had been conducted, there would still be the problem of how an appropriate international authority could obtain custody of these many terrorists-in-training without employing military force. It would have been necessary for the agents of an appropriate authority to locate these people somewhere in the hills and caves of Afghanistan, arrest them, and deliver them to an appropriate jurisdiction. Frankly, I can't quite believe in the feasibility of such an operation. And even presuming that many were arrested, thousands more would remain, all dedicated to anti-American and anti-Western violence. So in the end, I remain skeptical that nonviolent means could have eliminated the bases of al-Qaeda in Afghanistan.

And so we arrive at the Standard Theory, with which everyone will be familiar. The September 11 attacks were shocking and wrong, they proved the existence of a serious terrorist threat to the United States, other Western nations, and the global economy, and that threat demanded a military response against al-Qaeda bases in Afghanistan—which was, of course, what actually happened. Along the way, there is much to object to. I dispute the rhetoric of evil and evildoers and the careless appeals to justice. I argue against revenge attacks and the cultivation of hatred toward an demonized enemy. I think justice requires impartial open tribunals. For both ethical and practical reasons, I deplore the compromise of civil liberties. I think we should take our talk of human rights seriously, but most of us have failed to do that in the present situation. I don't like the "rally round the flag" effects of appeals to patriotism, and I find it frightening that Western countries are pressed to engage in a prolonged "war" against terrorism that could legitimate expansive U.S. militarism for the indefinite future. I regret what appear to be compromises to the sovereignty of my own country, Canada, as it answers calls to support the United States with regard to homeland security, fighting in Afghanistan, and a possibly expanded campaign against an "axis of evil." But despite all this, I can't seriously deny the central claims of the Standard Theory.

So why do I think it's important to discuss these other Theories—Zion, Internal Collusion, Roosting Chickens, and

Gandhian Internationalism? It's not that I agree with any of these theories; it's that I agree with John Stuart Mill about the importance of dissent. That's why I think it's highly regrettable that there was so little serious public discussion of these alternative accounts. They raise questions that need attention and arguments that need evaluation. Our understanding of the struggle against terrorism and its context could be greatly improved if we seriously engaged in this debate. We could gain a sense of complexity and ambiguity, and an appreciation for uncertainties. We could better articulate our own values and understand the limitations of our commitment to them. And we could arrive at a better perspective on gains and losses and on short-term successes and long-term problems.

Were there credible and consistent warnings of these attacks? Who ignored them and why? What's going on in intelligence services? Can they be reorganized to do a better job? Should aspects of U.S. policy in the Middle East be revised? Has the U.S. role in the conflict between Israel and the Palestinians been a constructive one? Should it be revised? Is dependence on Saudi oil desirable for the United States and other Western countries? Are there workable alternatives to that dependence? Can international institutions be developed to administer elements of criminal justice and identify terrorist acts as crimes, as distinct from causes for international war? Can we usefully cooperate with moderate Muslims to further education, democracy, and the capacity for critical discussion in Islamic countries? Can we distinguish between fixed values that we should not relinquish and policies based on tradition or expediency? Can some of the latter be constructively changed?

I have my own ideas on some of these questions, but that's not the point. I'm writing here not to propose answers but rather to defend the value of questions. Like John Stuart Mill, I sincerely believe that by raising and responding to questions we can best defend a free and open society.

Notes

John Stuart Mill's defense of freedom of expression is given in his classic work *On Liberty*. Charles Brisard and Guillaume Dasquie are the authors of *Bin Laden: La Vérité Interdite,* which is a major source of the Theory of Internal Collusion. A summary of their arguments was put forward by V. K. Shashiknar of New Delhi on November 21, 2001, and circulated on the Internet by war resisters. This summary emphasizes the story of John O'Neill. A version of the Internal Collusion theory is also defended by Johannes B. Koeppl, a former German defense ministry official and advisor for former NATO secretary General M. Werner. Comments by Koeppl were circulated on the Internet by Michael C. Ruppert, writing for From the Wilderness Publications (http://globalresearch.ca/articles/RUP11B.html). Accounts of John O'Neill's career and struggles are also given in Lawrence Wright, "The Counter-Terrorist: An FBI Agent's Obsession with al-Qaeda," *New Yorker,* January 14, 2002, 50–61; this account does not use O'Neill's story as evidence of Internal Collusion. Highly relevant considerations are also put forward in Thomas Powers, "The Trouble with the CIA," *New York Review of Books,* January 14, 2002, 28–32. The story of the Dubai hospital was also circulated by Michael C. Ruppert writing for From the Wilderness Publications. The argument about timing has appeared in various quarters and was publicized by Barrie Zwicker on Vision TV (Toronto) in mid-January 2002. The question of factors in the Muslim world that may have inhibited its advance is explored by Bernard Lewis in *What Went Wrong? Western Impact and Middle Eastern Response* (New York: Oxford University Press, 2002). The Roosting Chickens theory was expressed by many people on the political left. It is described, but not advocated, by Christopher Hitchens in "Stranger in a Strange Land: The Dismay of an Honest and Honorable Man of the Left," *Atlantic Monthly,* December 2001, 32–34.

More could be said about the theory of Internal Collusion. For a sustained argument, see Gore Vidal, *Dreaming War: Blood for Oil and the Cheney-Bush Junta* and *Perpetual War, Perpetual Peace* (New York: Nation Books, 2002). In its rhetoric, the George W. Bush administration often linked Iraq to al Qaeda and the September 11 attacks, though no such link could be demonstrated. Due perhaps to its emphasis on that connection, some critics tended to give more credence to collusion theories regarding the September 11 attacks. This is not my stance: I believe these matters are genuinely distinct. There is convincing evidence that persons in the George W. Bush administration had agreed on the need to defeat the Saddam Hussein regime even before taking office and were determined to do so, whatever the reactions of other countries and the U.N. Security Council; there was considerable deception and manipulation regarding these matters and the aftermath of the invasion of Iraq was appalling; none of these points, however, support collusion theories about the attacks of September 11.

13

LIFE

What is life? What is the value of a human life? What do you lose when you lose your life?

Epicurus once wrote that death cannot be a loss for the person who dies. He said, "Death is nothing to us, since so long as we exist, death is not with us; but when death comes, then we do not exist. It does not concern either the living or the dead, since for the former it is not, and the latter are no more." Epicurus wanted his philosophy to be helpful in the quest for human happiness. He offered this argument because death is deeply disturbing to most people, and he wanted to offer a kind of consolation to those who must die—meaning, of course, everyone. The implication was that we should cultivate the joys of life while we can.

Epicurus believed that after a person dies, that person no longer exists, in this world or anywhere else. The dead are no longer conscious and experience nothing. I will someday die. I might suffer while dying—perhaps I will die of a highly unpleasant and painful disease or experience agony when injured in an accident or a terrible attack—and such suffering is something to fear. But fearing death itself does not make sense; my death cannot be a loss for me because I will never experience it. Some people think Epicurus proved his point. But for others, the argument poses a deep puzzle:

It challenges the common belief that death is a loss for people who die as well as for their families and friends.

Certainly that's the perspective assumed in the "Portraits of Grief" series in the *New York Times*. Descriptions of the victims tell of so many good things these people were doing, one of the points being that having had their lives cut short on September 11, they would not be doing them any longer. Anthony Rodriguez, who dreamed of becoming a firefighter, was in a probationary class at the Fire Academy in New York. On September 11, he died trying to rescue others. His picture suggests a muscular build and a look of commitment. Rodriguez had served in the navy and as a mechanic and contractor before undertaking training as a firefighter. He had a wife, several stepchildren, a three-year-old son, and a daughter born September 14. Mary Stanley also lost her life at the World Trade Center on September 11. A vice president at Marsh and McLennan, Stanley was a devoted and loyal friend who became the family breadwinner after her husband developed serious health problems. She was a technology whiz at work and at home. Her photo shows her keen-eyed and smiling, vibrant with life and energy. A third portrait is that of Kenneth Swenson, a youthful vice president at Candor Fitzgerald and according to his wife, Leslie, a man of peaceful disposition and a great father to their two sons. Swenson spent his Saturday nights volunteering as a medical technician in the emergency squad in Chatham, New Jersey, where he lived with his family.

Loved and needed by many others, these people are profoundly missed. These deaths constitute an enormous loss to their families, friends, and communities. Although I didn't know any of them, by reading their stories, I begin to sense that loss. Reflecting on these portraits, I have a sense of something being cut off. There was so much potential here, so much talent, energy, love, and capacity for good. So much these people were doing, and could have continued doing, as life partners, parents, friends, workers, and volunteers.

And they were doing these things with commitment and zeal, enjoying life, soaring along. Then . . . they died and simply ceased to exist. It's as though I were watching a bird in flight and it suddenly disappeared, leaving the blue sky blank.

Against Epicurus, Thomas Nagel argued that our deaths deprive us of the experiences and opportunities we could have if we had lived longer. Nagel claimed that such deprivation is quite real even though it is never experienced by a dead person who, being dead, cannot experience this or anything else. The person who is deprived and who loses when he or she dies is the very person who lived, died, and lives no longer. If I were to die tomorrow, I would be deprived of many joys in life because I would no longer exist to experience them. Who would be deprived? I would. I who existed before my death and after it exist no longer. That I have been deprived of many experiences would be a reality—and that reality would persist even after my death. Contrary to what Epicurus argued, the loss of life is a real loss for the victims, not just for their friends, relatives, and communities.

It seems to me there's something right about Nagel's account, and it seems to fit the stories of people who were killed on September 11. Because he died on September 11, Anthony Rodriguez did not live to see his youngest child, born on September 14. He will never enjoy holidays and vacation trips with his children, watch them in playgrounds, see them graduate from high school, or reach his goal of being a New York City firefighter. When Anthony Rodriguez lost his life, he lost all these opportunities for challenge and experience.

Death cuts us off from every experience life has to offer. Every bowl of hot soup, steaming cup of coffee, funny movie, intimate conversation, swim, or walk on the beach. Every moment of curiosity, flash of understanding, hug and act of love. Every pleasure, every pain. All these experiences and joys of life are lost, resulting in a profound deprivation.

Would Nagel's ideas apply to every human life? Not every life is full of joy; there are the painful parts, too. The portraits in the *New York Times* were selective, after all: Those killed must also have experienced pain, anxiety, frustration, failure, and quarrels with loved ones. For some, suffering and grief outweigh happiness and life is miserable. Could the loss of one's life in such cases amount to something positive? If I believed that, on balance, my future life would be miserable for me and its loss would be nothing to regret and even be desirable, I might be led to commit suicide. I might seek to end my life in despair because nothing it could offer would ever outweigh my misery. Would someone be doing me a favor if he killed me under those circumstances? To this question, most people will answer a categorical "No." Some will qualify their response to say, "Only if you asked that person to do it." Even though some people may choose to die, the point about the morality of killing is that such a choice should be one's own. If someone kills me when I have not asked him to do so, he has done me a grievous wrong. Without my consent, he has cut me off from everything life has to offer.

Like the victims of the September 11 attacks, most of us are leading our lives, endorsing and completing projects and commitments, seeking fulfillment in education, vocations, travel, and relationships. We want to go on doing what we're doing. If we're cut off in midflight, we'd like to determine when and why and how and where. When people die, unless they are very old, we tend to feel sorry for them—sorry that they will miss the experiences and possibilities that life offers. When a disease or an accident strikes, we can't choose whether and when to die; and there's nothing to be done about that lack of choice. But killing is something else, something we seek to regulate by moral and legal codes. Killing is wrong because to kill another person, to cut off a life in progress without the consent of the person whose life it is, imposes on him or her a choice that no human being is entitled to make for another. Moral strictures against killing find their source in a central human value, that of life itself.

Leslie Swenson's favorite memory of her husband Kenneth involves balloons: Kenneth Swenson once released balloons of many colors over a football field where their sons were playing. He told his wife he had ordered them for her. I thought of those balloons when I saw a striking picture from postwar Afghanistan. Beside the bare frame of some structure, against a landscape of sand and rubble, stands a rugged-looking man. Dark-haired and bearded, wearing loose pants and a diamond-patterned vest, he looks to be in mid-adult life. This man holds a large bunch of balloons whose blue, red, and yellow contrast sharply with the dusty and devastated background. There's a strange beauty to the scene. I wonder about this man's situation—presumably, he wants to sell the balloons and he has an opportunity to try because of the defeat of the Taliban regime, which opposed such frivolities. And perhaps that was part of what the photographer sought to convey. An accompanying text explains that the picture was taken in a neighborhood of east Kabul and the wrecked structure is what remains of a building in a fairground. Because the area had been cleared of land mines, this balloon vendor was able to pass through it.

But where did he obtain the balloons? Who would be his customers, and what would be their circumstances? How would anybody have the money to buy balloons in the middle of all this devastation? I see only the picture and have no means of solving these small mysteries.

It's hard to know what happened in Afghanistan during and after all the bombing. Pictures and stories about American victims of the September 11 attack appear in many magazines and papers, but we hear little about the Afghan people and their lives. Early in the bombing campaign, when the Taliban were in power, we saw televised pictures of injured children in hospitals and homes in rubble. Taliban officials displayed them to the world in an attempt to buttress their case against America, citing them as proof that a campaign, based on rage about the loss of American lives, was oblivious to the value of these other lives. U.S. officials argued that such pictures were nothing but propaganda—and even critics of the bombing would probably have agreed that the U.S. Department of Defense was a more credible source of information than the Taliban. Outside observers had no way of knowing what was going on. In October and November, the British Broadcasting Corporation showed many shots of Afghan refugees huddled in tents against the cold and reported urgent appeals for donations by UNICEF, Doctors Without Borders, and other humanitarian organizations. The images were heartbreaking. These people were living in desperation. But you couldn't blame it all on bombing by Britain and the United States: millions of Afghan people had fled earlier, due to drought, conflicts between brutal warlords, and the cruel repression of the Taliban.

How many people were killed in the antiterrorist bombing of Afghanistan by Britain and the United States? How were families coping with these losses? How many of these people were innocent of any involvement in terrorism? How would people go on with their lives in the rubble of this shattered country? I try to imagine these people and the lives they are leading or want to lead. But it isn't easy.

Marc Herold, who teaches economics at the University of New Hampshire, made an effort to track Afghan casualties. Herold tried to follow media reports from around the world about civilian casualties in the bombing campaign. He estimated in January 2002 that some 4,000 Afghan civilians had been killed. Herold acknowledged that his figure was culled largely from unverified reports. At about the same time, Human Rights Watch estimated at least 1,000 civilian deaths. Another estimate was as high as 18,000. We will never know for sure how many Afghan civilians died. But it is plausible to believe the numbers will be substantial when bombs of weights ranging from 500 to 2,000 pounds are dropped on urban areas. When the Soviet Union occupied Afghanistan, Soviet commanders located military sites in residential and downtown districts, and Taliban forces later used these bases. Thus civilian and military resources were hard to separate. Assuming the goal was to destroy the Taliban's military resources, it seems that bombs had to be dropped on these civilian areas. Even presuming determined efforts to avoid killing civilians, some casualties would have been unavoidable.

Estimates of civilian casualties do not include military deaths. Asked what should be done about Taliban or al-Qaeda forces on the roads in mid-December, U.S. Defense Department Secretary Donald Rumsfeld said frankly, "You shoot them. If they're the kind you want to shoot, you shoot them." The *Frontier Post* claimed the Northern Alliance forces massacred 1,700 Taliban fighters twenty kilometers east of Kabul as they were advancing toward that city in mid-November 2001. By late January, reports indicated at least 1,000 Taliban and al-Qaeda men had been taken prisoner by the United States. Probably many thousands more were killed or injured—and we will never count their numbers.

Although stories of the victims of September 11 have been widely told, we see and hear little about the suffering of the people of Afghanistan. Their deaths are mostly uncounted and wholly depersonalized. There is good reason to believe that this selective attention is no accident. Marc Herold reports that the U.S. government is said to be spending millions of dollars to buy the exclusive rights to accurate satellite images of bombarded areas. Such images might permit commentators and critics to calculate more precisely the damage to Afghanistan and its people, estimations surely relevant to public assessments of the justifiability and value of the bombing campaign. Herold decided to attend to the issue of Afghan civilian casualties because of his underlying suspicion that modern weapons are not as precise and "smart" as military spokespersons would like Western citizens to believe. It's understandable that governments waging modern wars and wanting a good reputation would like to hide civilian casualties from the public eye. But when we hear so much about Western losses and almost nothing about losses far away, we risk losing all moral perspective on the conflict.

We can't fully comprehend what is lost when another person dies because we are unable to feel another person's experiences and sense of life. But when I see the pictures and read descriptions of people who were killed on September 11 in New York or Washington, D.C., I can begin to imagine the projects to which they were committed, the lives they led, and the joys they will miss. It's more difficult when I try to contemplate loss of life in Afghanistan. People who were killed there must have had aspirations for their lives and for their children's lives. They must have experienced some of life's pleasures: the savory taste of curry with a warm nan bread, the sweet smell of a newborn baby's head, an orange sunset above the sand, a cooling breeze on a hot summer day.

These people lived within a culture and historical experience different from my own. They spoke a language foreign to me and lived within the norms of a religion I do not understand. Their material lives were radically different from my own. All this poses challenges when I try to reflect on the lives they lost. But it doesn't negate the value of their lives or the tragedy of the losses in Afghanistan. I have little to assist me if I try to personalize the people who died. It's as if these poor and brown-skinned victims in faraway countries were not supposed to count; they have been given no face.

And yet from a moral point of view, these losses are every bit as serious as losses in North America. Just because we haven't counted the number of deaths or made a serious attempt to personalize these lives does not prove that they had no value. The imbalance in our sensitivity to victims risks a lack of perspective amounting to arrogance and disrespect; it suggests that our lives matter and theirs do not. It's an implication that plays straight into the hands of anti-American propagandists, who claim that Americans care only about the lives of their own people and not one whit about those of poor people living in Muslim countries.

We claim to believe that all human beings have a right to life. The United States, Britain, Canada, France—indeed all Western countries—are signatories to the United Nations Declaration of Human Rights, which proclaims, "All human beings are born free and equal in dignity and rights. They are endowed with reason and conscience and should act towards one another in a spirit of brotherhood. . . . Everyone is entitled to all the rights and freedoms set forth in this Declaration, without distinction of any kind, such as race, colour, sex, language, religion, political or other opinion, national or social origin, property, birth or other status. . . . *Everyone has the right to life, liberty, and security of the person.*" Through this proclamation, we claim to accept the principle that every human life has a special worth and dignity; that each human being—man, woman, and child—merits respect and treatment as a person with reason, a conscience, and a capacity for moral action. The human right to life is proclaimed to hold regardless of nationality, race, sex, religion, or any other such factor. Human beings have been granted this right on the basis of their humanity.

The right to life is the most fundamental of all human rights for the very simple reason that without it all other rights lose their significance. Afghan civilians have a right to life equal to that of any North American or European, or any other human being, anywhere. We should take those rights seriously and conduct ourselves accordingly—which entails conducting our foreign and economic affairs as if those rights really matter. Clearly, such conduct is not a reality. It's so far from being a reality that one can barely contemplate what it would mean in practical terms. But it's a central ideal, and one to which the international community has committed itself. It's also one we should try to live by.

To chat with Kant and Socrates would be delightful, but I don't expect to experience any such thing in a world after death. I expect to die; and after my death, I expect to be dead, and I expect the same for the victims of violence. Experience, logic, and science lead me to doubt that we are destined for better lives in another world where we can somehow compensate for our earthly losses and misfortunes. I believe that human beings find their experiences and challenges in this present world, not another one. We are not sure what happens to the consciousness of a person whose human brain is burned to dust or bombed into rubble, but in all probability consciousness is simply over. We have no evidence or logic to support the idea that somehow this person becomes wholly different, a heavenly sort of being who can somehow sustain consciousness without a physical body while still retaining a personal identity with the earthly human original. When I seriously consider it, we see little to support the hypothesis of a post-terrestrial world. That we live and die in this world are the realities to be respected.

Whatever one may think about the prospects for an afterlife, we know that we are human beings who have present lives to live and present problems to address. Political documents such as the UN Declaration of Human Rights have been adopted to guide our laws and institutions in the present world, which is the world we are coping with and the only world we know. That declaration was not designed to adjudicate arrangements in some speculative heaven or hell. It was founded on the reality that every human being is leading a human life and may have experiences and projects within it. The certainty of present life, the certainty of death, and the unlikelihood of an afterlife lend urgency to the right to life. There is more than rhetoric here: These rights should be respected.

Unlike Epicurus, I believe that death is a loss for the person whose death it is. Like Epicurus, I don't believe in immortality. I believe in mortality; I think death is really something that happens to human beings. For me, it's the reality of death that makes the right to life so important. Killing people is wrong because it deprives them of life, which is the necessary foundation for everything they could experience or accomplish in this world, the only world we know.

Whether it's yours or somebody else's, don't take life lightly. Make the best of it, savor it while you've got it, do your utmost. When it's over it's over—and this is why it matters so much.

Notes

The story of Anthony Rodriguez appeared in the *New York Times* "Portraits of Grief" series for January 6, 2002. Those of Mary Stanley and Kenneth Swenson appeared in that series in the December 23, 2001, edition of the paper. The oft-quoted comments of Epicurus on death are from his "Letter to Menoeceus," in *The Philosophy of Epicurus,* ed. George K. Strodach (Evanston: Northwestern University Press, 1963). A representative collection of recent philosophical thinking about death is that of John Martin Fischer, *The Metaphysics of Death* (Stanford, Calif.: Stanford University Press, 1993). Thomas Nagel's article, "Death," appears in that volume. The photograph of the balloon vendor was taken by Simon Norfolk and printed in the *New York Times Magazine,* January 6, 2002. Marc Herold's estimates of Afghan civilian casualties, and other estimates by Human Rights Watch, were reported in the *Globe and Mail* (Toronto) on January 3, 2002, and in the *New York Times,* February 10, 2002. His comments about his quest were reported in the *Globe and Mail* article.

When I tried to check figures for civilian casualties in Afghanistan in January, 2004, Marc Herold's work remained the standard source of information. He was cited as estimating 3,073 such deaths between October 2001 and May 2003, with some 5,531 serious injuries during that period. One source, 'Unknown News' (http://www.unknownnews.net/casualties.html) decried the dearth of further information on the topic. It seems that no one was attending closely to this crucial issue. Estimates of 100 U.S. troops killed and 300 seriously injured were offered at the site. Another estimate was 8,000 Afghan troops killed and some 24,000 Afghan troops seriously injured.

14

VINDICATION

Insult accompanies many injuries. When someone seriously injures us, he's not only damaging us, he's humiliating us, conveying the message that we don't deserve anything better. When we've been wronged, we often feel resentful and angry about the mistreatment and seek vindication. "Vindictiveness" and "vindication" have the same etymology: Both come from the Latin verb *vindicare*, which means "to claim, to set free, or to punish." Despite their historically common root, these words have different meanings today. Vindictiveness is connected with revenge; people who are vindictive try to get even by committing equally serious wrongs against those who injured them. Vindication, on the other hand, means showing oneself justified in the face of some challenge. The word "vindication" previously referred to revenge or punishment, but the dictionary lists those meanings as obsolete; now "vindication" means justification, a meaning that dates from the late seventeenth century. In this sense, a man whose writing abilities had been insulted would feel himself vindicated if he published a critically acclaimed novel. In committing serious wrongs, perpetrators have implied that their victims are worthless beings who deserve no more than injury and insult. Victims who seek vindication in the aftermath of wrongdoing are trying to disprove that message.

Writing about revenge, Susan Jacoby emphasized the distinction between vindication and vindictiveness. To illustrate her point, Jacoby recounted the powerful story of the Auschwitz survivor, Samuel Pisar. One of the youngest people ever sent to Auschwitz, Pisar survived partly because he lied about his age. After the war, he made his way to Australia, where an uncle gave him a home and a good education. He became a lawyer specializing in international law and devoted his life to cooperation and peace-related causes during the cold war. When I read Pisar's autobiography, I had the impression that all his adult life he had felt the profound moral insult of Nazi denigration, and I found that enormously sad. But Pisar's response to the deeply felt insult was far from tragic: he was determined to prove the Nazis had been wrong to treat him as a completely worthless human being. Pisar never expressed hatred toward Germans as a nation or a group; rather, he used his education and professional accomplishments in the interests of peace, seeking to further constructive engagements between the United States and the Soviet Union during the cold war. Pisar sought vindication, not revenge, and in doing so, he labored through his adult life to demonstrate his own value as an intelligent and productive human being.

Jacoby says that Pisar's moving story illustrates the old saying that "the best revenge is a life well-lived." But at this point, she seems to forget her own important distinction between vindication and vindictiveness. The interesting thing about Pisar lies precisely in the fact that he worked so hard and so effectively to vindicate himself without ever being vindictive. He never sought revenge. The life he lived so well was a substitute for revenge, not a form of it.

In a quest for vindication, two sorts of strategies are available. The first is "putting down" the wrongdoers; the second is "raising up" the victims. The putting-down strategy involves our imposing pain and suffering on those who hurt us, the idea being that by punishing them we demonstrate the wrongfulness of their actions and the merits of our own position. Because we are humiliated and insulted, we respond punitively by imposing suffering on the others and assume that by such actions we can prove our own merit. The humiliation or punishment of opponents can be satisfying to contemplate and shows them that the actions penalized were wrong. Punishment does have its purposes—and some may feel that victims are best vindicated when perpetrators are punished. Still, I suspect the punitive approach comes closer to vindictiveness than to vindication.

How can the suffering or humiliation of perpetrators demonstrate the dignity and worth of victims? Indeed, when the worth and dignity of victims has been challenged, it's hard to see why putting the perpetrators down should pull the victims up. There's something peculiar in this logic. We won't be better, or become better, or even seem better as a result of having made other people suffer. Nor can we demonstrate our own human merit by treating our enemies as if they lacked human merit. Vindication requires something more positive. That was Samuel Pisar's approach.

In her *A Vindication of the Rights of Woman*, Mary Wollstonecraft sought to justify rights that had been challenged by others by answering allegations that women were too frail and frivolous to deserve a role in public life. Wollstonecraft argued that women are creatures of reason who possess capacities for moral and intellectual development; and thus they have a legitimate claim to education and political participation. She had used the word "vindication" in the title of her earlier book, *A Vindication of the Rights of Men*, in which she defended the rights claimed by French revolutionaries against conservative critics such as Edmund Burke. Wollstonecraft didn't seek to vindicate women by putting down men. She didn't argue that men had no rights or capacities; she didn't launch a vendetta against Jean Jacques Rousseau and other writers who argued at self-indulgent length that women should be no more than the nurturers of children and the charming helpers of men. Instead, Wollstonecraft claimed for women capacities of understanding and action that could be positively developed if they enjoyed opportunities for education and employment outside the home.

What's needed for the vindication of a society is a hard look at our own values. What are we defending, in defending our way of life? What are we doing, and why? Values are the key to positive vindication.

What are these values? They are the significance and high value of human life. The right to life, founded on the dignity of persons and their capacity for moral choice. The belief in human rights, including the rights of women to be counted as free and equal human beings. The rule of law, which means that no party is exempt from the requirements of law and every person is presumed innocent until proven guilty and has a right to due legal process, including legal representation and a right to appeal. Tolerance of racial, religious, and ethnic differences. The separation of church and state, founded on the conviction that state power should not favor any one religion over any other. Freedom of conscience, thought, and expression, as matters of individual right. The intellectual and social value of an open society in which dissent is allowed and genuine inquiry can occur.

You could say these are American values—but that's misleading in an important way. They are Western values, inherited from theory and practice stemming from the dialogues and debates of ancient Athens, the religious struggles of the Reformation, the science and philosophy of the seventeenth century, the Enlightenment of the eighteenth century, and the American and French Revolutions. These values were crudely assaulted on September 11 and are threatened in its aftermath. Radical Islamists appeal to a different tradition and deny the value of scientific inquiry, the separation of church and state, secular law, human rights for women, and religious toleration and pluralism. To vindicate ourselves, we need to demonstrate a commitment to the core values given to us by our intellectual and political predecessors.

How can we do it? Early advice from President George W. Bush seemed to be "shop and fly"—as if a stock market propped by consumer spending would vindicate the United States and its allies and the best way of being a good citizen was to use your credit card liberally. Going to New York as a tourist and spending as much money as possible would help defy the terrorists, especially if you took a flight in order to get there. Governments could make points by going ahead with such events as the World Economic Summit and the Olympics. It's true that the importance of jobs and the economy can't be denied, and that international meetings and events have a role to play. But I don't think this is the route to vindication because it's not the core of the matter. The challenge is to acknowledge our fundamental values and comply with them in our own actions. At the very least, that means we should behave decently and fairly and do our utmost to conform to our own professed principles.

A country seeking to reassert itself after a destructive attack might look for a military victory and use its physical dominance to conquer and humiliate the enemy. We can see evidence of this result in photographs of the prisoners at Guantanamo Bay. There they are: enemy fighters in shackles, dressed in strange orange suits, heads and beards shaved, kept in cages, made to walk with their heads bowed, escorted to interrogations by armed soldiers. By having these men in custody and being able to interrogate them at length, the United States may have prevented further damaging attacks on itself and other nations. Perhaps many lives have been saved. And to some, the capture and humiliation of these people may have felt like a worthy revenge. But my sense is that the Guantanamo situation did not provide a positive vindication for the United States. Far from it. The punitive humiliation of these prisoners inspired considerable criticism at home and abroad. "They are down, so why aren't we up?" That is the core of the matter: we don't bring ourselves up by bringing someone else down.

If we seek to defend a society and way of life supposedly grounded on principles of the rule of law by violating core principles of international law as articulated in the Geneva Conventions, the means used are contrary to the ends professed. If we disregard the basic civil liberties of thousands of suspected terrorists and millions of resident foreign citizens and announce our willingness to detain them indefinitely without charge, we have lost our credibility as defenders of human rights. Nor can we demonstrate respect for freedom of conscience by criminalizing thinkers sympathetic to the ideas of Osama bin Laden and radical Islam. Such contradictions expose serious problems about means and ends.

On this topic, Gandhi's reflections during the long struggle for Indian independence are especially fascinating. Gandhi argued against the idea that the end justifies the means. He asserted that we control our immediate means but we do not control the consequences of our actions and policies. If we fail to conform our means to our values, we fail to apply them in the only context in which it is possible to apply them; in effect, that means giving up on our values altogether. "Means are, after all, everything," Gandhi said. He also argued that if we employ means contrary to our ends, we will always defeat ourselves in the long run because the ends we reach will be characterized by the means we used to get there. For Gandhi, this relationship of means to ends was a major reason for using nonviolent means in the political struggle for Indian independence. He believed that a violent revolution would only lead to a violent postrevolutionary society, and this wouldn't amount to an improvement over colonial oppression. Gandhi also pointed out that the character of people and their institutions is affected by the means they choose. People who commit acts of discrimination learn to discriminate; those who commit acts of violence learn to practice and condone violence. The history of violent revolutions over the last fifty some years offers little to refute these ideas, and the continuation of a viable democracy and the rule of law in India more than fifty years after its nonviolent achievement of independence suggests a powerful argument in their support.

President George W. Bush has sometimes spoken of defending Western civilization against terrorism. In a few incautious comments, the president even alluded to crusades. Such comments recall the theory of Clash of Civilizations put forward by Samuel Huntington, who interprets global politics as a struggle between starkly opposed civilizations—Islam being one, Western Judeo-Christian civilization another. An objection urged by many critics is that the Huntington theory underemphasizes the differences within traditions while overemphasizing the differences between them. Another objection is that by believing that such clashes are inevitable, we might actually cause them to occur. Huntington's ideas were widely discussed before September 11 and he has resisted attempts to interpret the attacks as a confirmation of his theory. But others have appealed enthusiastically to the Clash of Civilizations account, contending a radical Islamist attack on such symbols as the World Trade Center and the Pentagon provides a perfect illustration of the theory. One recent commentator went further than the Huntington thesis, suggesting that the contemporary West is like Rome during its fall and that the terrorists can be seen as barbarians at the gate.

Barbarians at the gate? A clash of civilizations? Aren't such conceptions a little on the melodramatic side? I feel compelled to respond by saying, hey, this is real life, not an adventure movie. We are not engaged in a global battle in which monolithic forces of good are arrayed against a monolithic "axis" of evil; rather, we are dealing with a many-faceted struggle against a network of terrorist groups and agents that is being played out against a complex background characterized by many ambiguities and contending political and economic interests.

And yet, for all the complexity, diversity, ambiguities, and contending interests, I do think that important values are at stake here. Islamic terrorists and their sympathizers not only oppose U.S. foreign and economic policy, they despise Western values and culture. And yet they have used Western technology, science, and economies for purposes of their own. Moving from country to country as immigrants, tourists, and students, they have exploited the traditions of civil liberties, available education, and toleration of differences. While benefiting from the dynamism, creativity, and multiculturalism of Western societies, they have at the same time denigrated them, in the starkest terms, as impure, degenerate, and alienated from the one true God. Western values and traditions have been exploited by terrorists—and no doubt potential terrorists will seek to exploit them in the future. But that's not to say we should give up. If we do that, we will have lost what we're trying to save.

When President George W. Bush said, "Either you're with us or you're with the terrorists," he posed a false dichotomy: obviously, there are other possibilities. A person can object to terrorism and terrorist killings without agreeing with every detail of the U.S. military campaign in Afghanistan; and all the more without agreeing to the proposed expansions of that campaign into other countries charged with being terrorist because they are hostile to the United States. When it comes to basic values, I find the "for or against" conception more tempting—though still oversimplified. I deplore the theocratic and antifemale ideas of radical Islamists. I don't for a minute accept the idea that texts from the seventh century offer reliable guidance for law and economics in the twenty-first. I cherish the Western values of human rights, rule of law, and freedom of conscience. I believe that Western values do need to be defended—

yes, vindicated—in the wake of the September 11 attacks. If I could believe that such fundamental values were truly a central concern of the U.S. administration, I'd be expressing wholehearted solidarity. The problem is, there's too much self-interest, hypocrisy, and inconsistency along the way.

In the wake of the September 11 attacks, the United States received expressions of sympathy from around the world, and it has been ready to use that sympathy to oppose terrorism by seeking international cooperation in the struggle against terrorism. Terrorism threatens global security and requires a cooperative international response; the building of the coalition could have been the beginning of a multilateral approach. Early on, commentators speculated that perhaps George W. Bush was shifting away from the resolute unilateralism that had previously characterized his thought and policy. But there was no general shift. Disappointingly, the United States played the cooperative role only when it was in its immediate interests to do so. And seeking multilateral support in a coalition against terrorism while behaving unilaterally in other important contexts does not enhance the credibility of the United States.

Terrorism is not the only threat to global security; and regarding other threats, the United States has been woefully unwilling to adopt a cooperative approach. Instead, it has behaved in a short-sighted and self-serving manner, resolutely putting its own narrowly construed interests first. It withdrew unilaterally from the 1972 Anti-Ballistic Missile Treaty. It walked out of a London conference seeking to strengthen a protocol for inspections regarding the 1972 Biological and Toxic Weapons Convention; it then later accused Iraq, Iran, North Korea, Libya, Sudan, and Syria of violating that convention. It opposed a United Nations agreement to curb the flow of illicit small arms. It continues to oppose efforts to establish an International Criminal Court. It stands against the 1997 Kyoto Protocol on carbon dioxide emissions and global climate change. So far as moral credibility goes, these uncoopera-tive approaches are absolutely unhelpful. They indicate a deep fail-ure of reciprocity.

Given the ways in which Western values have been exploited by terrorists, preserving them in the context of ongoing threats pres-ents an enormous challenge. It's a difficult problem and I don't doubt that tough choices will have to be made. Still, I think certain things are clear. Heedless unilateralism will inspire resentment and make people question your credibility. Bullying and bribing won't be enough to win friends and influence people. Shopping and fly-ing won't demonstrate the value of a way of life. You don't vindi-cate yourself by putting down someone else. Most important of all, violating your own principles is no way to defend them.

Notes

The idea that wrongdoers morally insult victims, implying that they merit no respect, is stated in Jeffrie Murphy and Jean Hampton, *Forgiveness and Mercy* (New York: Cambridge University Press, 1988). My idea that vindication should involve a positive as opposed to a punitive response is defended in chapter 1 of Trudy Govier, *Forgiveness and Revenge* (London: Routledge, 2002). Information about "vindication," "vindictiveness," and their Latin root in "vindicare" is taken from the *Compact Edition of the Oxford English Dictionary.* Susan Jacoby's book is *Wild Justice* (New York: Harper and Row, 1983). Samuel Pisar tells his own story in *Of Blood and Hope* (Boston: Little Brown, 1979). Mary Wollstonecraft's "Vindication" may be found in *Mary Wollstonecraft: Political Writings* (Oxford: Oxford University Press, 1994). Samuel Huntington's book is called *The Clash of Civilizations and the Remaking of the World Order* (New York: Simon and Schuster 1996). The analogy to the fall of Rome is in Michael Ignatieff, "Barbarians at the Gate?" *New York Review of Books,* February 28, 2002. An articulation of central American values, along the lines of what is called for here, is offered in Jean Bethke Elshtain, *Just War Against Terror: The Burden of American Power in a Violent World* (New York: Basic Books, 2003). Samuel Huntington's book is called *The Clash of Civilizations and the Remaking of the World Order* (New York: Simon and Schuster, 1996). In "Looking the World in the Eye," *Atlantic Monthly,* December 2001, Robert Kaplan explains why Huntington is unwilling to apply his theory directly to the events of September 11. The analogy to the fall of Rome is found in Michael Ignatieff, "Barbarians at the Gate?" *New York Review of Books,* February 28, 2002.

15

HOPE

Hope is not a matter of certainty or confidence; it's a belief in positive possibilities. When we hope for some outcome, we don't expect it in the sense of believing that it will come to pass. Rather, we think it is possible—or even likely, if other things go well. Hope is emotion as well as belief, because when we hope for an outcome, we desire it and regard it as good. Emotionally, hoping is somewhat like wishing, but more closely tied to the realities of the world. What we hope for we regard as possible, even though it is not yet real. In contrast to hopes, wishes need have no such connection to reality—for instance, an elderly woman might wish that she were young again.

The Stoics believed that hope was delusory and dangerous, illustrating only too well our baneful tendency to attach ourselves to events beyond our control. They advised that to achieve tranquillity we should restrict ourselves to caring only for things within our power. Epictetus the Stoic taught that hope is objectionable because it sets us up for disappointment. According to the Stoics' deterministic conception of reality, what happens in the world is fully fixed, and we can't do anything about it. To hope for something merely possible would be as absurd as hoping that 2 plus 1 might someday equal 7. Training in philosophy would let us see the interlocking pattern of the universe, and when we did, we would understand the irrationality of believing in an open future that allows positive possibilities to become realities. The Stoics understood philosophy as a kind of therapy that would rid us of irrational feelings—hope being one of these.

I believe the Stoics were wrong about hope. The universe is not fixed inevitably by fate or some inexorable chain of causes; there is a genuine sense in which the future is open. Furthermore, in some respects, the future can be affected by human choices and actions. Our beliefs, feelings, and attitudes affect the world in complex ways, and the situations we help to produce rebound in turn to affect us.

Writing before the Stoics, Heraclitus of Ephesus said, "He who does not expect what cannot be expected will not make the unattainable attainable." By this somewhat puzzling statement, I think Heraclitus meant that unusual things happen, contrary to our expectations—and it's only by taking account of such possibilities that we can reach goals that we might have dismissed as impossible. In other words, it's our sensitivity to surprises that supports our determination to work for novel outcomes. Heraclitus seems to have been in favor of hope.

Optimists believe confidently and positively—often blithely and brashly—that good things will come. They assure us, yes, everything will be all right in the end. One example of a blithe optimist in this sense is a leader who assumes that social ills can be countered by military strategies and refuses to consider arguments to the contrary. Optimists are often accused of being naïve, and if they refuse to acknowledge good evidence of corruption, environmental depletion, and other threatening phenomena, they really are naïve. But hope is not the same as naïve optimism; hopeful attitudes do not presume that good outcomes are somehow guaranteed. Rather, hope is based on the assumption that good outcomes are possible, though not certain, and hope is compatible with the acknowledgment of obstacles standing in the way. For example, some people hope for a more democratic United Nations Security Council while recognizing that the veto power given to five permanent members is significantly undemocratic, will be difficult to amend, and constitutes an obstacle to reform.

Questioning often supports hope; when we question dogmas about inevitability and impossibility, we may discover positive possibilities rejected in orthodox thinking. Imagination can support hope too, by helping us envision what those desired possibilities would amount to in real terms and what means we might use to work towards them.

Some people manage to make the "impossible" into a reality. My own favorite example is that of Tracey, a young woman who is blessed with a beautiful soprano voice. Tracey took singing lessons, and I heard her give a spectacular performance of a difficult Mozart aria at a private recital. There was something a little unusual about her, something I couldn't quite place. When I inquired, her teacher told me that Tracey was profoundly hearing-handicapped. She understood speech mostly by lip-reading and sometimes missed social cues; this could make her seem odd and posed difficulties in some social relationships. In fact, Tracey had been unable to continue choral singing as a result of this social awkwardness. She had not taken music lessons as a child, did not know how to read music when she came to this teacher, and tuned herself by feeling the vibrations of a tuning fork. Somehow, against all odds, she had reached the level of this wonderful performance.

I like to think of Tracey as creeping through the premises of an apparently irrefutable argument. "Deaf people can't sing; you are deaf; therefore you can't sing." Questioning orthodoxy led Tracey to resist the idea that singing would be impossible for her, and her imagination led her to create her own unique ways of learning. This young woman wanted to sing, believed it was possible for her to learn, hoped for success, resolved to learn, sought teaching, and discovered ways to compensate for her disabilities. Her hope was based on a strikingly firm sense of positive possibility. And her hope was active rather than passive: She must have worked very hard to achieve that performance I heard. I don't know how she did it and I can't precisely locate the mistakes in the apparently convincing "proof" that her achievement was impossible. Part of the explanation must be that there are various forms of deafness, appreciating music, and learning to sing, and our common understanding of what it is to sense sound and appreciate music is oversimplified. Another factor must be that this young woman was incredibly determined—and she did have a good voice.

The presence or absence of hope is something that influences us profoundly because hope affects our interpretation of the world and the goals we pursue within it. Tracey believed in a possibility that many would have dismissed and used her imagination and energy to find a means to achieve her goal. Intellectually, imaginatively, emotionally, and actively, she committed herself to her hope. Her story proves that determined practical hope is more than wishful thinking. And it should serve as a warning to all who assert with dogmatic confidence that something is simply impossible. Which is not to say, of course, that people who try hard enough can do anything they want—Tracey's story doesn't prove that. But it is to say that it's worth questioning dogmas about impossibility. Just because something is not yet actual doesn't prove that it's impossible; nor does our not having succeeded so far prove that we never will. Institutions such as a fairly administered International Criminal Court and a World Trade Organization that fully protects workers' rights to unionize would no doubt be difficult to achieve, but that doesn't prove they're impossible.

The point that what we believe we can do affects what we can in fact do is highly relevant in all this. Dogmatic beliefs can become self-fulfilling when they lead us to ignore new strategies and alternatives. It's not only dogmatic, but counterproductive to believe categorically that problems will always have the structure they have today. For example, many people assume uncritically that individualized transportation in the industrialized world must involve the consumption of fossil fuels and dependence on Middle East oil, necessitating a Western domination of that region. Yet alternative approaches to transit can be developed by people who make the effort—and many are already doing just that. The same sort of point can be made about nonviolent responses to political conflicts. The belief that such means are impossible is not proven by the fact that they don't exist now. Accepting such a belief is counterproductive as well as unwarranted because it prevents people from even trying to develop positive alternatives to the status quo.

The point that negative dogmas can be counterproductive enough to make themselves true may be easier to grasp in circumstances closer to our individual lives. Consider doctors and medical diagnosis, for instance: doctors are sometimes criticized for denying their patients grounds for hope. What would you say about a doctor who tells her patient quite categorically that he only has six months to live? First, you could remind her that even such people as doctors have been known to make mistakes. The medical knowledge she employs and its application to a particular patient are open to question, and for that reason what she says cannot be an absolute certainty. Second, you could raise the issue of a self-fulfilling negative prediction. It's a demonstrated fact that attitudes have a significant impact on health, and a patient told in no uncertain terms that his disorder is incurable may become so depressed that he contributes to his own demise. Some years back, Norman Cousins was told by a doctor that he had only a few months to live. He rebelled, prescribing for himself a heavy dose of laughter—and laughed himself to years of further life. Then he wrote a book, *Anatomy of an Illness*, offering an explanation of why the approach had worked for him.

So should a doctor always hold out hope—even when the best available medical knowledge provides strong evidence that her patient will die soon? At what point does hope shade into self-deception? It's a tough question; but at the very least, doctors can avoid implying certainty by qualifying their pronouncements with phrases such as "so far as we can tell" and "unless I'm missing something." Whether it's medicine or international relations, conflict resolution or restorative justice, a lack of dogmatism never hurt anybody.

A doctor once told me that I had a "chronic life-threatening disease." The implication was, put your health before everything else; whatever you do, don't take on any stressful obligations. Exercise, diet, doctors, and pills—these were to be my future. She was warning me, just as many doctors warn their patients, and she no doubt had her reasons. A counselor told me later that doctors are taught this sort of communication strategy in medical school: "Scare the daylights (or something less polite) out of them; it's the only way to make them follow our advice." Good patients are "compliant," which, in this model of the world, is a positive personality trait meaning that one will follow doctors' orders. Because few people are willing or able to be good patients in this sense, and many tend to be overly complacent about such matters as weight and blood pressure, doctors try to frighten people in an effort to persuade them to be obedient. But this doctor read me wrong: I'm not inclined to complacency; on the contrary, I'm a bit of a worrying type. And I resent it if I think I'm being manipulated.

Fortunately, my doctor's discouraging words brought forth the rebel in me (not to mention the philosopher). To me, the notion that the sole or primary goal of life would be maintaining it in the context of a "chronic life-threatening disease" was not only uninspiring but more than slightly insane. Striving all the time to preserve your health so you could go on living to go on striving to maintain your health so you could go on living? It seemed crazily negative. Life is worthwhile and meaningful because of our participation in the world—our goals, projects, relationships, and experiences. To have no goal save to go on keeping yourself alive would be absurd. Well, she's a doctor, not a philosopher; and thinking about the meaning of life, and in particular, the meaning of my life, is not her job. It is, however, my job—and I was determined to follow Tracey's lead and creep through her premises to go ahead with determination and hope.

Hope isn't some kind of happy sensation inside people's minds or heads; it's an attitude that profoundly affects who we are, how we understand reality, what we do, and how we shape our world. Believing that good outcomes are possible affects the way we interpret people and events and encourages us to seek opportunities and work for the results we want. Political violence, war, and terror are not known to be inevitable features of the human condition. They are common and they are terrible and many people assume they are inevitable, and that makes them hard to resist. But it doesn't prove they are irresistible in any absolute sense. There are better ways to respond to conflicts, and if enough people believe that and work for it, we may be able to create institutions to assist with the task. The thousands of people who work for international nongovernmental organizations (fondly known as INGOs) must have hope in spades. Doctors without Borders, for example, sends volunteers to wars, refugee camps, and natural catastrophes. I see them on television and feel amazed by their idealism, commitment, and energy. Like their colleagues in the Red Cross, UNICEF, Save the Children, and literally hundreds of other organizations, they work from attitudes of hope and convey that hope to others.

The opposite of hope is despair. When we despair, we feel no basis for hope and have no hope. Despair, of course, has profound emotional elements. But it involves beliefs as well: It's grounded on a conviction that things simply cannot get better. It's a woeful dogmatism. The logic of despair requires us to prove "there's only one sort of thing that can happen, and it's bad." The logic of hope, on the other hand, requires a commitment to the statement that "there are many things that can happen and some of them may be good"—a claim that is far easier to prove. In other words, the claim that bad things are certain (despair) is harder to demonstrate than the claim that good things are possible (hope). It's a wonderful result: logic itself favors hope rather than despair.

Immanuel Kant was the philosopher who most strongly urged the significance of hope. Like the Stoics, Kant valued reason and independence and was no advocate of emotionality or blithe optimism. Again like the Stoics, and unlike many thinkers of his own time, he was no blithe optimist avowing confidence in the inevitability of human progress. Kant experienced poverty and hardship, lived for some years in a city occupied by Russian soldiers, and he knew of appalling violence during the French Revolution. He believed that human beings have an enduring capacity for evil as well as good. Nevertheless, he argued that human history and human life must be lived with a hopeful attitude. Kant insisted that human progress is always possible and that it is only by firmly believing in this possibility that we will be able to act on our moral obligations. For moral reasons, we must take the rights and dignity of our fellow human beings into account; these really are our moral obligations, and if we are to act according to them, we must believe that it is at least possible that what we do can contribute to a better world. Improvements in the world will come about only from the morally motivated actions of individual men and women who trust in each other's commitment and work determinedly for better institutions. Such commitment requires hope that human history is ultimately shifting in a progressive direction and a moral world order can become a reality.

It was in 1795 that Kant wrote his essay "Perpetual Peace: A Philosophical Sketch." There he argued that eventually human beings would find the costs of war so great that they would have to look for something better. Conflicts between states would occur; reasonable human beings would continue to seek solutions.

Eventually, motivated by moral conviction and a resolute hope for a better world, some would work out a nonviolent response through international law and a world federation of states that had come together to provide for human dignity, respect, and sustainable peace. There is a shift in this work from pessimism (ongoing conflict) to optimism (confidence in the power of reason), and then from optimism to hope (active commitment to the possibility of better institutions). Some people read "Perpetual Peace" as a strange utopian dream, a work not to be taken seriously because it was the product of Kant's old age, when his mental powers were declining. Others find his cosmopolitan vision poignantly relevant to our own times. I am one of these. When serious crimes are committed by persons of many nationalities against many other persons of many other nationalities; when such crimes involve communications, economies, and travel around the world; and when they have a dramatic impact on many of the world's people and nations, it is clear that a genuinely multilateral international response is required. Workable institutions for law and conflict resolution are desirable, and for more than theoretical reasons.

Ultimately, Kant believed, human survival requires the establishment of a sustainable peace. In the long run, human rights cannot be protected by violent means—thus the idea of "perpetual peace" gains practical relevance. Improving the human condition by principled means is something that is set for us as a task, Kant said. There's no guarantee that a task we begin will be completed in our lifetime, so we have to trust that other human beings who live after us will continue the labor that we have begun. Kant's defense of hope was based on his conviction that moral principles must accompany us when we move from the private sphere into public life. "A true system of politics can therefore not take a single step without first paying tribute to morality," which can "cut through the knot which politics cannot untie." Politics is not some unique realm where violence is inevitable and morality doesn't matter.

Forms of realpolitik that seek power without moral foundation, implying that idealistic commitment is only a matter of theory and not relevant to practice, must be rejected as untrue to life. Such conceptions, Kant warned, are particularly damaging because they "may themselves produce the very evil they predict." Despite the ills of the world and the human capacity for evil, Kant was inspired by hope to proclaim that "evil will not have the last word either in one's own heart nor in history."

So far as moral action within human history is concerned, it's crucial to believe in the possibility of improvement, which is just to say that hope is necessary for human endeavor. Without that form of expecting the unexpected, that commitment to making progress possible, we can make no sense of our obligations and actions. Whether it's the French Revolution of the eighteenth century or the war against terrorism in the twenty-first, events in history don't interpret themselves. It is we who interpret events—and we can do that with varying degrees of dogmatism, skepticism, hope, or despair. Within limits, we shape history by the interpretations we endorse and the values and principles on which we act.

To act morally in the complex world of politics, we have to believe there is some point in doing so. Anyone who would act morally in human history needs hope in the sense of a practical conviction that unexpected solutions may be found, progress is possible, and our efforts may contribute to a better world. We don't need certainty, and it would surely be naïve to think we've got it. But we do need the hope that we may someday come together as co-citizens in a world where we manage our affairs according to the principles of morality and law.

Are human beings doomed to be simplistic militarists issuing threats and brandishing weapons, reducing buildings to rubble and rubble to dust, seeking security in domination, striving to vanquish foreign evils while refusing to acknowledge those at home? Devastating the planet that should be a shared home for all humankind? Are we no more than a group of fools headed for inevitable disaster? Kant asked that question and conceded that evidence could be cited to support an affirmative answer. But that's not quite the issue. The point is that for practical reasons, even if we have evidence suggesting such a view, it would be utterly counterproductive to accept it. We can't assume generalized folly and inevitable catastrophe and make moral sense of our lives at the same time. Living as political beings requires the hope that better things may come.

Notes

The Stoic attitudes to emotions are elegantly explained by Martha Nussbaum in *The Therapy of Desire* (Princeton: Princeton University Press, 1994). A convenient anthology of Stoic writings is *Essential Works of Stoicism*, ed. Moses Hadas (New York: Bantam Books, 1965). The fragment from Heraclitus is taken from John Burnet, *Early Greek Philosophy* (New York: World Publishing Company, 1930). The full title of Norman Cousins' book is *Anatomy of an Illness as Perceived by the Patient: Reflections on Healing and Regeneration* (New York: Norton, 1979). Kant's essay on perpetual peace may be found in *Kant: Political Writings*, ed. Hans Reiss (Cambridge: Cambridge University Press, 1970). Quotations by Kant are from "On the Common Saying: This May Be True in Theory, But It Does Not Apply in Practice" (1793); and "Perpetual Peace: A Philosophical Sketch" (1795). I discuss hope in contrast to pessimism, optimism, and cynicism in the final chapter of *Social Trust and Human Communities* (Kingston and Montreal: McGill-Queen's University Press, 1997).

INDEX